P9-APF-709

FLORIDA STATE
UNIVERSITY LIBRARIES

SEP 12 1997

TALLAHASSEE, FLORIDA

The
Economic
Pivot in a
Political
Context

The
Economic
Pivot in a
Political
Context

CHARLES WOLF JR.

With a foreword by **Newton N. Minow**

TRANSACTION PUBLISHERS
New Brunswick (U.S.A.) and London (U.K.)

*HC
59.15
W65
1997*

Copyright © 1997 by RAND.

All rights reserved under International and Pan-American Copyright Conventions. No part of this book may be reproduced or transmitted in any form or by any means, electronic or mechanical, including photocopy, recording, or any information storage and retrieval system, without prior permission in writing from the publisher. All inquiries should be addressed to Transaction Publishers, Rutgers—The State University, New Brunswick, New Jersey 08903.

This book is printed on acid-free paper that meets the American National Standard for Permanence of Paper for Printed Library Materials.

Library of Congress Catalog Number: 97-3693
ISBN: 1-56000-326-X
Printed in the United States of America

Library of Congress Cataloging-in-Publication Data

Wolf, Charles, 1924–
    The economic pivot in a political context / Charles Wolf, Jr. ; foreword by Newton N. Minow
        p. cm.
    Includes index.
    ISBN 1-56000-326-X (alk. paper)
    1. Economic history—1990– . 2. International economic relations. 3. Economic policy. 4. United States—Economic conditions—1981– . 5. United States—Ecnomic policy—1993– . 6. Military policy. 7. Competition, International. I. Title.
HC59.15.W65 1997
338.973—dc21   97-3693
                                                                         CIP

This is a RAND study.

RAND books are available on a wide variety of topics. To obtain information on other publications, write or call Distribution Services, RAND, 1700 Main Street, P.O. Box 2138, Santa Monica, CA 90407-2138, (310) 393-0411, ext 6686.

Contents

Acknowledgments

Chapter 1. Edited version published as "The Fine Art of the False Alarm," *The Wall Street Journal*, November 1, 1994.

Chapter 2. Edited version published as "The Coming of the Neo-Classical World," *The Wall Street Journal*, February 23, 1996.

Chapter 3. Edited version published as "The New Mercantilism," *The Public Interest*, no. 116, Summer 1994.

Chapter 4. Edited version published as "Taking on the Global Gurus," *The Wall Street Journal*, May 1, 1996.

Chapter 5. Edited version published as "How Do We Force Ourselves to Save More?" *The Los Angeles Times*, August 11, 1996.

Chapter 6. Published in *Business Economics*, vol. 31, no. 3, July 1996, pp. 7–10. An abridged version was published as "Private Money Gaining as Chief Economic Fuel," *The Los Angeles Times*, December 3, 1995.

Chapter 7. Edited version published as "The Dollar Depreciation Mystery," *The Wall Street Journal*, February 10, 1995.

Chapter 8. Edited version published in *The Wall Street Journal*, July 7, 1995. Review of *The End of the Nation State: The Rise of Regional Economies*, by Kenichi Ohame.

Chapter 9. Abbreviated version published as "Why Asia-Pacific Holds the Cards," *The New York Times*, January 17, 1993.

Chapter 10. Edited version published as "Us Against Us," *World Monitor: The Christian Science Monitor Monthly*, April 1993.

Chapter 11. Edited version published as "The Limits of Trust," *The National Interest*, no. 41, Fall 1995, pp. 95–98. Review of *Trust: The Social Virtues and the Creation of Prosperity*, by Francis Fukuyama.

Chapter 13. Edited version published as "When Too Much Agreement is a Danger to World Stability," *The Los Angeles Times*, August 8, 1995.

Chapter 14. Abbreviated version published as "Money and Might— Policy Handmaidens," *The Los Angeles Times*, May 6, 1991.

Chapter 16. Edited version published in *Korean Journal of Defense Analysis*, Winter 1994.

Chapter 17. Abbreviated version published as "Arms Transfer: A Trade That Needs Policing," *The Wall Street Journal*, March 16, 1992.

Chapter 18. Edited version published as "U.S. Arms Exports Can Backfire," *The Wall Street Journal*, June 21, 1994.

Chapter 19. Abbreviated version published as "The State of the World," *The Wall Street Journal*, February 4, 1992. Review of *Seize the Moment: America's Challenge in a One-Superpower World*, by Richard Nixon.

Chapter 20. Edited version published as "Beyond Cold War: Peace and Turmoil Zones," *The Wall Street Journal*, August 30, 1993. Review of *The Real World Order: Zones of Peace/Zones of Turmoil*, by Max Singer and Aaron Wildavsky.

Chapter 21. Edited version published as "Demystifying the Japanese Mystique," *The New York Times*, May 26, 1991.

Chapter 22. Edited version published as "U.S.-Japan Trade Platitudes," *The Asian Wall Street Journal*, January 13, 1994, and in *The Wall Street Journal* as "Wrong Way to Talk About Trade," February 10, 1994.

Chapter 23. Edited version published as "It's the Current-Account Deficit, Stupid," *The Wall Street Journal*, July 6, 1993.

Chapter 24. Edited version published as "Strong Yen, Weak Economy," *The Asian Wall Street Journal*, July 27, 1994.

Chapter 25. Edited version published as "Stimulating Japan's Economy, Not Tariffs, Will Open Up Its Markets," *The Los Angeles Times*, June 11, 1995.

Chapter 26. Revised version published as "How China Grew Overnight," *The Wall Street Journal*, November 16, 1993.

Chapter 27. Edited version published as "Yin, Yang of Yuan and Yen," *The Wall Street Journal*, December 5, 1995. Review of *Asia Rising: Why America Will Prosper as Asia's Economies Boom*, by Jim Rohwer.

Chapter 28. Edited version published as "In the Shade of the Rising Yen," *The Wall Street Journal*, March 21, 1995. Review of *Japan: Who Governs?*, by Chalmers Johnson and *The American Economy*, by Nicholas Spulber.

Chapter 29. Abbreviated version published as "Friction-Filled Future for 'Big Three,'" *The Wall Street Journal*, August 12, 1992. Review of *A Cold Peace: America, Japan, Germany, and the Struggle for Supremacy*, by Jeffrey E. Garten.

Chapter 30. Edited version published as "Getting to Market," *National Interest*, Spring 1991.

Chapter 31. Abbreviated version published as "Less Pain, More Gain for the East Bloc," *The Wall Street Journal*, November 19, 1990.

Chapter 32. Abbreviated version published as "Yeltsin's Choice—Democracy and Free Markets," *The Wall Street Journal*, June 3, 1992.

Chapter 33. Abbreviated version published as "Reasons for Economic Optimism in Ex-U.S.S.R.," *The Wall Street Journal*, January 3, 1992.

Chapter 34. First published as "Reasons for Hope," *World Monitor: The Christian Science Monitor Monthly*, January 1993.

Chapter 35. Abbreviated version published as "Independence for Ukraine and Russia," *The Wall Street Journal*, November 29, 1991.

Chapter 36. Abbreviated version published as "Soviets Need Change, Not Tons of Money," *The Los Angeles Times*, September 12, 1991.

Chapter 37. Abbreviated version published as "An Aid Package for Russia—Beyond Clinton's," *The Wall Street Journal*, April 16, 1993.

Chapter 38. Abbreviated version published as "Sweepstakes Capitalism," *The Wall Street Journal*, July 12, 1991.

Chapter 39. Abbreviated version published as "Latin-Style Swaps for Russia," *The Wall Street Journal*, November 19, 1992.

Foreword

The art of creating a well written, closely reasoned, persuasive and coherent essay is in danger of disappearing today. That is why the reader is so grateful that Charlie Wolf's excellent op-eds have been collected and preserved in this new book for permanent reference and intellectual nourishment. The current shortage of thoughtful discourse on tough public policy issues shows that sometimes the law of supply and demand doesn't work. Although there is plenty of citizen demand for balanced analysis and commentary, the supply these days in missing in action.

As Charlie explains in his prologue, almost all of his essays have appeared in print over the last six years in important and distinguished publications. Two appear in print for the first time because otherwise competent editors considered their arguments either too tame or too wild. You can judge for yourself the wisdom or taste of these editors. I suggest they were not used to such high quality.

Politics and economics are thought to be separate and separable disciplines. Charlie knows better, and so will you when you read and understand his explanation of the two types of conventional wisdom—and appreciate why he prefers one type over the other.

Newton N. Minow

Prologue

Conventional Unwisdom
and Unconventional Wisdom

A Reader's Guide

There are two types of conventional wisdom. One type consists of wisdom that has become conventional because it is valid. The other type is (erroneously) assumed to be valid because it has become conventional. Most of the chapters of this book reaffirm and sometimes extend the first type, or expose and explode the *un*wisdom of the second type. Occasionally, too, I suggest why and how the latter can be corrected.

The thirty-nine essays in this book were, with two exceptions, published between the end of 1990 and the middle of 1996 in *The Wall Street Journal, The Los Angeles Times, The New York Times, The Public Interest, The National Interest, The Christian Science Monitor,* and *The Korean Journal of Defense Analysis.* The two exceptions are chapter 12, "'Downsizing,' Corporate Responsibility, and the Tradeoff Between Efficiency and Equity," written in July 1996, which was judged by two editors to be too tame to be published, and chapter 15, "Economics and Security in Central Europe," written in 1994 and co-authored with former Secretary of Defense Harold Brown, which two other editors judged to be too wild to be published.

The chapters cover a variety of subjects—some large and some small, some relevant to policy and some not, some addressing domestic issues in the United States and others addressing international issues, some dealing with global matters and others dealing with particular countries and areas, especially Japan, China, and Russia. Most of the chapters deal with various types of interactions within these subjects: interactions between economics and politics, between economics and security, between domestic and international economies, and between theory and policy.

To assist the reader in navigating through these crossing currents, I have grouped the thirty-nine chapters into four reasonably coherent parts: Part I, Economic Forecasts and the Changing Global Economy; Part II, Economic Power and Military Power; Part III, The Economies of Japan and China; and Part IV, Transforming the Russian and Ukrainian Economies.

Despite their diversity, most of the chapters reflect a similar approach and style of analysis. That approach is conveyed with reasonable fidelity by the book's title, *The Economic Pivot in a Political Context* (for which I am indebted to Irving Louis Horowitz). In viewing the variety of subjects, policy issues, and interactions addressed in the book, I generally focus on one or another economic fact, theory, or assumption (the "pivot" in the title), thereafter elaborating and relating it to the political and policy domain (the "political context" in the title) to which it applies. The reasoning and supporting evidence that connects the "pivot" to the "context" is generally nontechnical, eclectic, and transparent. While this process may strike some readers as more congenial and convincing than it does others, it should help readers to identify where and why they disagree with me, or where and why I diverge from the conventional wisdom.

This approach has both advantages and limitations. Where the advantages appear to dominate (which I hope is more frequent), the result is to expose the "unwisdom" that is often conventionally accepted, or to suggest new insights, or "unconventional" wisdom, that may apply in these various domains.

The New Political Context

The post-cold war political context is much harder to characterize than its predecessor. The cold war, despite its noxious character, had the advantage of structure to go along with the manifest disadvantages of its real or presumed threats.

In this structured context, it was usually clear (more or less) who was on which side of particular international disputes or conflicts, and why. What is conventionally referred to as the "post-cold war environment" lacks such a structure. Yet, there seem to be certain defining attributes of the emerging global environment, which provide a broad political context within which the economic "pivots" operate. The defining attributes of this emerging environment seem to me fourfold: complexity, volatility, permeability, and domesticity.

By *complexity*, I mean that there are more players or actors in the international arena than there used to be. There are not only more countries than those that inhabited the cold war space, but also more multilateral organizations, more regional and subregional groups, more multinational corporations and international business alliances, more financial institutions and networks, and more nongovernment organizations and "quasi"-nongovernmental organizations. So, the new environment is more complex.

By *volatility*, I mean that the emerging environment is characterized by more change and a more rapid rate of change, by more uncertainty, more current and potential "contingencies" and greater instability, than there used to be. These contingencies often occur at quite different levels of violence and intensity (examples in recent years include Haiti, Somalia, Iraq, Kurdistan, the West Bank, Chechnya, the Taiwan Strait, the Spratly and Senkaku-Diaoyu Islands, and so on). So the emerging environment is less predictable.

By *permeability*, I refer to the increased openness of the international environment—openness to the flows of information, trade, capital, technology, and people. As a result of the information revolution that has occurred and continues to gain momentum, a perpetual transnational dialogue goes on through the Internet. Negotiations among the increased number of players—in business as well as governments—have become global and diurnal, rather than localized and periodic. So the global environment has fewer barriers. "Iron curtains" have been replaced by porous ones.

By *domesticity*, I mean that, notwithstanding the three preceding characteristics of the new environment, there is within the U.S. in particular and in other countries more generally, a greater preoccupation with and priority accorded to *domestic* social, political, and economic issues. These include economic growth, employment, education, health care, social equity, civil justice, environmental standards, crime, and substance abuse. Although many of these "domestic" concerns are affected by developments in the international arena, these effects are often indirect or delayed. As a result, the heightened priority accorded to domestic policy matters is often at the expense of attention to international affairs. Yet, this shift of priorities isn't properly termed "isolationism." Indeed, the increased permeability of the international environment carries with it more international contacts, linkages, and transactions. Nevertheless, some reordering of priorities, attention, and resources toward domestic affairs and policies, rather than foreign and defense policies, is characteristic of the new environment.

There is evident tension among these several forces and characteristics, and their resultant is by no means clear. My hunch is that the resultant is probably more benign than malign. Consequently, most of the chapters reflect a mood of moderate optimism about the international economy and the position of the United States in it. However, while this optimism is encouraged by the increased permeability that I referred to, it is also bounded by the attributes of volatility, complexity, and domesticity whose constraining effects are clearly reflected in other chapters.

Themes, Conclusions, and Prejudices

Several principal themes are developed, or at least touched upon, in the various chapters:

1. One theme, perhaps more relevant to readers interested in social science methodology than in policy, is reflected in the frequent references that are made to the unreliability of assessments and forecasts made by duly-credentialed social science experts. These include political scientists, sociologists, historians, and regionalists, as well as economists. This theme is reflected in chapter 1 on "Nonaccountability Among the Experts," chapter 4 on "Glib Rhetoric, Loose Thinking," chapter 26 on "China's Enlarged Economy," chapter 28 on "The United States and Japan," and elsewhere. It recalls the satirical comment of Nobel laureate Paul Samuelson, when he observed some years ago that, "Economists have correctly predicted seven of the last four recessions"!

Actually, my treatment of this theme goes farther than Samuelson's in several respects: for example, in targeting other social scientists besides economists, in identifying broader subjects than recession forecasts where presumed social science experts have badly erred (e.g., in asserting the decline of the American economy and the ascendency of that of Japan, in predicting the "free-fall" of the Russian and Ukrainian economies). Moreover, it is typically the case that these experts absolve themselves of any obligation to acknowledge their errors. The result is a surprising degree of nonaccountability that is presumed to leave intact their prior reputations for expertise.

2. Another recurring theme, as well as a reason for optimism, concerns the ebb of what I refer to as "neo-mercantilism." This is addressed in chapter 2 bearing that title, chapter 3 on "Pitfalls of Public Policy," and in several of the essays dealing with the Japanese economy and its relation to that of the U.S.

Mercantilism was a protectionist economic doctrine advanced in the eighteenth and nineteenth centuries that advocated state action to promote specific exports, to protect domestic industries, and to generate trade surpluses. It was given a new cachet in the 1970s and 80s through the so-called "new trade theory" developed by academic economists, such as Paul Krugman and Laura Tyson, and popularized by various commentators, including James Fallows, Chalmers Johnson, Clyde Prestowitz, and Karel van Wolferen. Formal economic concepts, such as economies of scale, and economies of learning, reinforced by the powerful example of Japan's economic accomplishments, enabled the "new trade theory" to provide the basis for what was called "strategic trade policy" and "industrial policy." These represented the "neo-mercantilist" analogues of the earlier mercantilist doctrines.

Neo-mercantilist trade policy and industrial policy were reflected in popular advocacy of policies favoring protectionism, subsidization and industrial "targeting"—that is, picking "winners" and "losers" as a goal of government policy. Fortunately, by the 1990s, these restrictive, neo-mercantilist policies have been overtaken by a rediscovery of the powerful stimulus to growth represented by economic liberalization and competition, both in domestic economic policy and in international economic policy. Consequently, in my judgment, the theme of neo-mercantilism's ebb and its prospective end bodes well for future economic trends and the evolution of the world economy.

3. One of the standard and reiterated beliefs about the general political context of the post-cold war era is that the relevance, role, and utility of military power has receded compared to that accorded to economic power. I think this belief is partly valid. However, it obscures as much as it reveals. More specifically, what it obscures are the key questions of how large the diminution in the relative importance of military power has been, and what kinds of military power matter more or matter less in the post-cold war context?

In fact, the diminution in the importance of military power relative to economic power has probably been considerably less than is commonly believed. Indeed, the continued importance of military power is reflected in the frequency with which it has been employed in the post-cold war environment—for example, in the Persian Gulf, Iraq and elsewhere in the Middle East, Bosnia, Chechnya, the Taiwan Strait, Haiti, and Somalia.

In the post-cold war context, the types of military power that matter most are those that can be employed rapidly, with precision and discrimination, based on detailed and accurate current intelligence. The changes that have occurred in the composition of effective military power are of no less significance than the changes that have occurred in the relative importance of aggregate military force.

This general theme, as well as several of its ramifications, including those relating to the international arms trade and how to control it, are addressed in the eight chapters of Part II dealing with economic power and military power.

4. Another of the themes, exemplifying the "economic pivot" unfolding in a political context, addresses the special problems posed by the Japanese economic "model" and the protracted economic frictions between Japan and the United States. These frictions have been due in part to the fact that Japan's economy has been managed as a modern mercantilist ("neo-mercantilist") endeavor through the favored treatment of key export industries and the restriction of access by foreign competition in the domestic Japanese market. While this process has surely produced benefits and progress for Japan, it has also created major problems and vulnerabilities in the Japanese economic system. The benefits were strikingly reflected in Japan's impressive growth record of the 1970s and 1980s. The problems and vulnerabilities have become no less strikingly evident in Japan's economic stagnation during the 1990s, as well as its severely weakened banking and financial industries, and the abundant examples of illicit transactions that have surfaced in real estate, finance, construction, and other sectors.

However, the frictions between the United States and Japan have been due principally to other factors besides Japan's mercantilism, more specifically to the macroeconomic imbalance between savings and investment in the U.S. economy. This imbalance is reflected in the perennial U.S. tendency to consume and invest more than it produces, to save less than it invests, and hence to import more goods and services than it exports, requiring that the U.S. import capital either in the form of direct investment from abroad or by foreign borrowing.

This analysis of the Japanese and U.S. economies and of the sources of friction between the U.S. and Japan is dealt with in detail in Part III, especially chapters 21, "Dissecting the Japanese Problem with 'Occam's Razor,'" chapter 22, "Resuming the Protracted U.S.-Japan Economic Debate," chapter 23, "Clearing the Fog Over U.S.-Japan Economic Relations," chapter 24, "The Strong Yen of a Weakened Economy," and chapter 25, "Sense and Nonsense About Dealing with Japan," as well as other chapters of Part III.

This same theme is also addressed from a different standpoint in chapter 5 of Part I dealing with "Taxes, Trade, and Growth." Here, the focus is on the importance of tax restructuring in the United States as a means of encouraging both savings and investment in the American economy. It is especially important that incentives be realigned so that savings are increased by more than investment, so that the perennial shortfall of domestic savings below domestic investment, which is reflected in the economy's current account deficits, can be reversed. Tax restructuring of the sort described in chapter 5 can contribute to boosting economic growth in the United States from about 2.5 percent per annum to about 3 percent or more throughout the next decade.

5. While the transformation of the Russian and Ukrainian economies is constrained by their respective political contexts, several of the chapters in Part IV suggest grounds for somewhat greater optimism about the progress and prospects of economic reform in those countries than has been characteristic of the conventional wisdom. Chapter 30, "Transforming Command Economies Into Market Economies," describes the ingredients required for thoroughgoing transformation of centrally planned "command" economies like those of Russia and Ukraine. Rather than the so-called "shock" therapy in these countries having been ineffective because it was excessive, these chapters suggest that instead the therapy was incomplete and insufficent. Some, but certainly not all or even most of the ingredients required for successful transformation of command economies toward market-based ones have been pursued. Still, the progress of privatization of the economy, through the rapid emergence of new entrepreneurs and through stock distribution of state enterprises, has been encouraging in Russia and Ukraine.

Moreover, while officially reported output has continued to decline, the so-called "grey economy" has been growing rapidly. This contrast is, to a considerable extent, attributable to the high rates and complexity of business taxation. As a result, business output and income are pervasively underreported to evade taxation. Netting out the growth of the grey economy, against the fall in the official economy, has not been done. If it were, my guess is that the net figure would be positive.

Hits and Misses

I have previously criticized the lack of "accountability" among the experts, because of their avoidance of comparisons between what they anticipated or predicted, on the one hand, and what actually ensued on the other. So, it is only appropriate for me to try to do better in assessing the chapters comprising this book.

Reviewing materials that have been written over the past five or six years can be a source of reassurance if the assessments turn out to have been accurate, or humbling if they have been wide of the mark. In fact, there are entries on both sides of this ledger—both "hits" and "misses." I think there have been considerably more of the former than the latter.

The assessments presented in Part III of the book dealing with the economies of Japan, China, and Asia more generally, seem to me to stand up quite well in the light of the actual record of events after these papers were written. However, the assessment that I made in 1993 (based on work done several years earlier) of China's growth rate of between five and six percent turned out to be an underestimate, while my estimate of Japan's growth—about two and a half percent annually—seems likely to be a slight overestimate.

Another "hit" relates to the assessment made in Part II dealing with the relation between economic power and military power. The reality of the post-cold war environment seems to confirm the assessment made in the chapters of Part II. There, I suggest that the precedence generally accorded to economic power over military power, while probably of the right sign, has been exaggerated as to its magnitude in most writings and commentary on this subject.

On the other hand, the forecast that I made of the scale of the international arms trade erred. The actual scale of this trade has turned out to be only half of what is envisaged in chapters 17 and 18. However, I would add the comment that several of the factors tending to sustain the international weapons market in the post-cold war era remain active and may still provide a source of worrisome growth in this trade.

Although I would argue that the grounds for my guarded optimism about the prospects of the Russian and Ukrainian economies retain validity, it is probably fair to say that the chapters of Part IV of the book underestimated the pain, costs, and time required for transforming the command economies of Russia and Ukraine into effective, market-based economies.

Another "hit" I would claim is the general picture of the long-term international capital market, and its prospective winners and losers. The picture that is painted in chapter 6 of Part I, "Global Competition For Long-Term Capital: Who Will Win?" seems to me still to be accurate. The market will be characterized by a relative growth of private relative to public capital flows. The "winners" in this competition will be those countries that sustain high levels of growth, that provide reasonable prospects for political stability, and a greater degree of predictability in their legal, regulatory, and general business environment.

Part I

Economic Forecasts and the Changing Global Economy

1

Nonaccountability Among the Experts

Academic social science is often treated dismissively, and with good reason: its standards of accountability are depressingly low. Seldom are errors acknowledged, nor are those responsible asked to account for them.

Three contemporary and well-publicized forecasts by highly credentialed social scientists exemplify this failure of accountability: the putative decline of the American economy, Japan's prospective dominance in the world economy, and the anticipated collapse of the Russian economy. In each case, the "findings" have been wrong. In none has there been an acknowledgment of error or recognition of a professional obligation to account for it.

In the late 1980s a mutually reinforcing group of social scientists, including Yale historian Paul Kennedy, and political scientists David Calleo of Johns Hopkins, and Robert Gilpin of Princeton, confidently, and sometimes exuberantly, predicted the impending decline of the American economy and of American power in the world economy. They ascribed this to "imperial overstretch" and the burden of excessive military expenditures associated with it. As supporting evidence they noted that U.S. industrial productivity lagged behind Japan and Germany, that the U.S. was becoming the world's largest debtor, and that the U.S. share of the global product had shrunk from more than 50 percent in the 1950s, to about 23 or 24 percent in the early 1980s while defense spending had risen to nearly 7 percent of the U.S. GDP.

From the start, the facts diverged from these claims. For example, the U.S. share of the world economy was atypically large in the 1950s and early 60s due to the obvious destructive effects of World War II on the economies of Europe and Japan. Typically, in the years prior to World War II, the U.S. represented only about a fifth of the world economy. Contrary to claims about the irrepressible rise of U.S. defense outlays,

3

defense spending actually peaked in 1986, two or three years before Kennedy and his colleagues reached their supposedly carefully researched conclusions; by that time, defense spending had already declined, both in constant dollars and as a percentage of the U.S. GDP. Finally, the U.S. lag in productivity growth was largely due to the economy's success in absorbing into the employed labor force large numbers of relatively low-skilled workers, as well as to serious flaws in the methods of measuring productivity, especially in service industries.

Today, the U.S. exhibits the most robust growth—about 3 percent annually—among all the world's advanced economies, its rate of productivity growth is equal to or above that of the others, and its share of the global product is about 24 or 25 percent (in purchasing power parity terms)—only slightly less than that of Japan and the European Union combined!

The social scientists who predicted the 1980s U.S. economic decline misunderstood the past, misinterpreted what was then current, and misperceived an immediate future that has now become current. Yet the authors of this mistaken history and of these mistaken forecasts never felt compelled to acknowledge their mistakes, nor did their academic colleagues feel it appropriate to call them to account. Such are the standards of accountability in the social sciences.

Contemporaneous with these mistaken forecasts about the U.S. was an equally erroneous set that proclaimed Japan's impending dominance in the world economy, thereby displacing the U.S. This prediction was accompanied by assertions that Japan's brand of capitalism was fundamentally "different" from that of the West, that its overwhelming competitive strength was due to the central direction exercised by its far-sighted bureaucracy, and that this system was impervious to reform.

The numerous sources of these opinions included political scientist-historian Chalmers Johnson from the University of California in San Diego, political scientist Stephen Cohen at U.C. Berkeley, economist Laura Tyson then at Berkeley and currently chair of the President's Council of Economic Advisors, and MIT economist Lester Thurow. Their views have been amplified and popularized by several others, including Karel van Wolferen, Clyde Prestowitz, and James Fallows.

Again, the facts diverged from these views. Contrary to them, Japan encountered a severe and protracted recession. Its annual economic growth since 1991 has hovered close to zero. In purchasing power parity terms,

Japan's GDP is now about one-third that of the United States, and somewhat less than that of China. The profits of Japan's nonfinancial businesses have plummeted, and the balance sheets of Japanese financial institutions have been seriously weakened by the decline in the market value of their assets. (If Japan's bank regulators were to apply solvency standards equivalent to those applied in the United States, the balance sheets and net capital of many of Japan's principal banks would be below, or barely in compliance with, accepted international standards!) Finally, the annual rate of growth in Japan's technological progress (what economists refer to as "total factor productivity") over the past seven years has averaged between minus two tenths of 1 percent and plus one half of 1 percent, compared to a rate of more than 1 percent in the United States.

This is not to suggest that Japan's economy will remain stagnant. Indeed, recent RAND estimates envisage annual rates of growth equal to or slightly above those of the United States for the remainder of this century. In the longer run, however, Japan will encounter severe problems from several basic structural difficulties that it faces: adverse demographic trends (Japan's population is aging more rapidly than that of the European Union and the United States, and the fertility rate of Japanese women is well below that necessary to maintain Japan's present population), gradually declining savings rates, an overvalued exchange rate, and a political system that is in disarray.

So, the predictions by social science experts of Japan's impending economic ascendance are no less wide of the mark than those of U.S. decline. Once again, the social scientists associated with this view of Japan ignore the evidence that conflicts with it, and feel no obligation to acknowledge or explain their mistakes.

The third striking instance of nonaccountability concerns the prevailing assessment by social scientists of the progress of economic reform in Russia. In recent years, numerous recognized experts on Russia with noteworthy social science credentials—including Wellesley economist Marshall Goldman, George Washington University political scientist Peter Reddaway, Harvard economist Jeffrey Sachs, and several Russian academicians like Larisa Piyasheva, Grigor Yavlinsky, and Boris Federov—have deplored the "freefall" of the Russian economy, its impending hyperinflation, and its likely "collapse." (Ironically, these pessimistic pronouncements recall the equally mistaken optimism about the Soviet

Union's economic performance that prevailed in the years preceding dissolution of the Soviet Union in 1990.) Explanations offered for the currently pessimistic assessments have differed among these experts: some have blamed too rapid reform ("shock therapy"), while others charged that the reform was too slow, and still others blamed corruption and crime, or fiscal irresponsibility, or regional fragmentation, or the personal vagaries of President Yeltsin.

Once again, the realities diverged from these assessments. Instead of collapse, there have been several positive accomplishments. Privatization has been more widespread and more successful than anticipated; currently, 50 percent of Russia's GDP is produced by private commercial entities. Inflation has been significantly reduced and most of the Russian federation's budget has been placed on a cash basis. Foreign direct investment has been steadily rising. Moreover, a reasonable *modus vivendi* has been worked out between the central federation government and its component regions.

To be sure, the Russian economy has not "turned the corner," and confidence in its future would be premature. Nevertheless, the alarmists have seriously erred. Once again, there is no acknowledgment of error. Instead, the shortness of memories allows, and indeed encourages, an absence of professional accountability.

As long as the social science professions eschew reasonable standards of accountability, others are well advised to view their pronouncements and publications as conjecture and opinion rather than scientifically based findings, and to discount them accordingly.

November 1994

2

The Ebb of Neo-Mercantilism

If or as the United States moves toward a balanced federal budget—probably accompanied by some restructuring of its tax code and by the increased parsimony of aging baby boomers to provide for their retirement—gross current savings in the United States will rise by perhaps 2 or 3 percent of the gross domestic product. The result will be to reduce (and perhaps reverse) the perennial U.S. deficits on current account—the amount by which U.S. imports of goods and services exceeds its exports, which is also about 2 percent of GDP. The powerful economic stimulus that these deficits have provided for the world economy will be gone. The rest of the world will have to import more from the United States if it is to export more to the United States. *Therefore, U.S. exports can be expected to rise.*

U.S. current account deficits, reflecting the relatively easy access of foreign exports to the American market, have not only provided a boost to the world economy. They have also facilitated a neo-mercantilist orientation of many policymakers in both developing and developed countries. This orientation views exports as somehow "better" than imports, domestic markets as warranting some forms of protection against foreign imports, and the export-dominated "Japanese model" of development as particularly meritorious. These views, which have persisted despite formal expressions of support for freer trade and more open market access, will have to change. Indeed, as difficulties are encountered in adjusting to the altered international economic environment, many of those who previously criticized the United States for its lack of fiscal "discipline"—ostensibly one of the contributory causes of its current account deficits—may come to view those bygone days with nostalgia.

This is not to deny that the U.S. has also benefited immensely from its current account deficits. Indeed, these deficits have enabled the U.S. to consume and invest more than it has produced. And, because the dollar is the world's principal reserve currency, the U.S. has been able to finance its debt in its own currency without appreciable adjustment costs. However, one of the perverse consequences of this symbiosis has been the diversion of much of the world's net savings to the United States rather than elsewhere.

The coming turnaround in the U.S. current account deficits doesn't imply that so-called "export-led" growth of other countries will become irrelevant. The incentives and competitive pressures imposed by global markets will remain essential and universal ingredients for sustained growth. But, while all countries can increase their exports, they can't do so unless they increase their imports, as well. In the aggregate, current account surpluses and current account deficits must sum to zero.

Of course, it is conceivable that other developed countries might assume the U.S. role of consistently absorbing expanded imports from the rest of the world, without commensurate increases in their own exports. This could act as an engine of growth for other countries in the same way that U.S. current account deficits have done in the past.

However, it is almost unimaginable that either Japan or the European Union will assume this role, although in 1995, Japan at least began to increase its imports by more than its exports, and thereby to reduce its global current account surplus for the first time in five years.

Barring this unlikely scenario, circumstances that have allowed if not encouraged the trade policies and so-called "industrial policies" of other countries to be equated with export promotion, will be fundamentally altered. The neo-mercantilist world of the recent past will move toward a more neo-classical world in the future. As the U.S. savings rate rises, its exports will rise relative to its imports. Developing countries that seek to sustain rapid rates of growth are likely to incur current account deficits, because their domestic investment will exceed domestic savings. Their imports from developed countries, including the U.S., will then exceed exports to them. Long-term, voluntary capital—in the form of foreign direct investment, portfolio equity investment, and privately financed credit—will flow from developed countries to finance the current account deficits of developing countries. Current account deficits financed by voluntary capital inflow to countries that are experiencing sustained and substantial economic growth, while maintaining sensible macroeconomic policies and reasonable price stability, should be recognized as a normal part of this neo-classical world. Intervention by an overly precautionary IMF "fire brigade" would not be warranted in such circumstances.

In this neo-classical world, exports will cease to be viewed as somehow "better" than imports. Instead, the primary purpose of exports will be recognized as a means of paying for imports, while the primary purpose of imports will be recognized as a means of accommodating higher rates of investment and growth than would otherwise be possible.

February 1996

3

Pitfalls of Public Policy:
Strategic Trade Policy and Industrial Policy

Ideas, Policies, and Defunct Economists

In one of his many insightful observations, John Maynard Keynes noted that "practical men, who believe themselves to be quite exempt from any intellectual influences, are usually the slaves of some defunct economist." He noted further that the power of ideas can be immense "both when they are right and when they are wrong," concluding that "it is ideas, not vested interests, which are dangerous for good or evil."

One of these currently captivating ideas is that aggressive government actions—including "strategic trade policy" and "industrial policy"—will bring about increased efficiency (the slogan is "competitiveness") of U.S. firms in international markets. It can be argued that Keynes's insight is wide of the mark in this instance because the principal sources of these ideas are not defunct, but alive, vigorous, articulate, and influential. They include such academic advocates as Paul Krugman at MIT, John Zysman at Berkeley, and Laura Tyson, formerly at Berkeley and currently chairman of the Council of Economic Advisors, and numerous well-known commentators and popularizers including Clyde Prestowitz, James Fallows, Chalmers Johnson, Pat Choate, and Karel van Wolferen. However, Keynes's original insight can be defended by a reasonable counterargument: antecedents to these current ideas can be traced to several "defunct" mercantilists of bygone centuries, including Jean Baptiste Colbert, Thomas Mun, Antonio Serra, Friedrich List, and Alexander Hamilton, who advocated state action to promote specific exports, restrict specific imports to protect domestic industries, and provide trade surpluses, gold bullion and, it was believed, enhanced state power.

"Strategic trade policy" and "industrial policy" differ from one another, in some respects. Strategic trade policy typically focuses on promoting specific exports and limiting specific imports. Industrial policy focuses on the development of key domestic industries, with international trade accorded a secondary role. Nevertheless, despite their differences, both policies share a fundamental premise: government can and should select certain industries, technologies, or firms whose advancement is of "critical" importance for the performance of the economy as a whole, and accord the selected ones some form of preferential treatment—whether through government subsidies, special tax advantages, restricting imports to protect domestic producers, or promoting exports by pressing the Japanese, or other trading partners to assure special market access for these critical products. To some, "critical" means "high technology" industries in general (Tyson); to others, it means semiconductors in particular (Fallows), or telecommunications, or automobiles, or machine tools, or even rice. In the interests of simplicity, and at a modest cost of precision, I will refer to both sets of policies as "preferential industrial and trade policies," or (PITP).

The appeal of PITP to many "practical men" (as well as some impractical ones), is understandable because there are reasonable theoretical arguments as well as empirical evidence and experience to support it. What is usually overlooked by those who accept the arguments for PITP is the existence of strong counterarguments, as well as indications that the usually cited evidence in support of PITP is at best ambiguous, and probably wrong. While the Japanese experience is usually cited in support of PITP, there is a simpler and more compelling explanation behind the Japanese story. Moreover, if a vigorous set of preferential policies were to be pursued in the context of the U.S. political system, there are strong reasons for expecting them to fail badly.

In the following discussion, I will first summarize the theory that provides support for PITP, next consider the theory's shortcomings, then elaborate a countervailing view, and thereafter suggest why efforts to implement such policies in a pluralistic, interest-group democracy like our own can be expected to generate costs and mistakes that exceed its potential benefits. Along the way, I will suggest that Japan's notable economic and technological accomplishments of the past three decades— notwithstanding a current recession that has been deeper and longer than that of the United States, and seems likely to continue in face of the U.S. recovery—are attributable to other reasons than those allegedly provided by Japan's own neo-mercantilist policies.

The Case for Strategic Trade Policy and Industrial Policy

The intellectual basis for STP rests on several well-established economic precepts: first, the concept of "economies of scale"—the notion that large firms can realize certain gains and efficiencies not accessible to small ones; and second, the concept of "economies of learning"—the notion that firms or individuals, or organizations, that have acquired abundant experience thereby become more proficient and efficient than less experienced entities.

A corollary of the gains associated with large size, and with accumulated learning and experience, is certain spill-over benefits ("externalities") that are presumed to accrue to the economy as a whole, or to other industries in addition to the advantages directly realized by the large and experienced firms themselves.

These externalities—benefits external to the firm or industry generating them, and not susceptible to its control or exploitation—may be of several types and may arise in various ways. For example, if a firm or industry achieves a large size, it may provide a large market that redounds to the advantage of feeder industries, firms, and suppliers. Thus, the large size of the automotive industry provides opportunities for electronics, tire, lighting, and other component producers that, in turn, enable them to increase their own efficiency through larger scale production. Economists refer to these spill-overs as "pecuniary externalities."

Another type of spillover—referred to as "technological externalities"—may result from the experience, learning, and accumulated know-how of the originating firm or industry, and the more highly skilled labor pool that is thereby created, with potential benefits for other firms or industries. The development and remarkable growth of the Internet system, as a result of linking computers and telecommunications, provides a striking example of technological externalities that hugely benefit international business, finance, and commerce.

The Effects of Size and Learning

Describing the importance of firm size, Laura Tyson asserts that: "In such ["technology-intensive"] industries, costs fall and product quality improves as the scale of production increases, [and] the returns to technological advance create beneficial spill-overs for other economic activities" (Tyson 1992). Economies of scale are typically represented by economists in the form of unit costs that decline as the scale of output, or its capacity, increases. Economies of scale are traceable to the increased opportunities of large firms for division of labor and specialization of tasks, and for spreading fixed costs over a larger volume of output as production rises. Thus, supermarkets typically can underprice small grocers and profit from doing so. And, at least until recently, it has been presumed that large-scale steelmakers, like USX or Kobe, can out-compete small steel producers because of the economies of scale that the larger firms can realize.

"Economies of learning"—that is, efficiencies resulting from accumulated experience—are also presumed to result in lower costs, and to yield a competitive advantage for more experienced firms that have been in business for a longer time. Economists typically use various proxies to measure the efficiencies that result from experience: for example, the cumulative output of individual firms, or the cumulative years they have been in business. The premise underlying these proxy measures is that the greater the cumulative output, or the greater the number of years of accumulated experience, the more proficient will be their operations, and the stronger their competitive position relative to that of less experienced firms. Thus, IBM, General Motors, and Toyota have been presumed—at least in the past—to derive a competitive advantage from their accumulated learning and experience relative to that of their competitors.

Economies of scale, and economies of learning, plus the corollary externalities with which they are associated, provide the intellectually respectable ideas that have led many "practical men" to accept the case for "strategic trade policy," and national "industrial policy." Because of economies of scale and economies of learning, it is argued, public policy should invoke one or another type of preference, or subsidy to "establish a lead in an industry, [and]…once this lead is established it becomes self-reinforcing and tends to persist." (Krugman, 1991.) Tyson refers to the "first-mover advantages" that can be realized by dominant firms and technologies (Tyson 1992).

So much for the theoretical arguments for strategic trade policy. The trouble with them is that there are equally convincing, although less familiar, theoretical arguments against them. There are strong theoretical reasons why large size and long experience may entail offsetting burdens, risks, and disadvantages.

This debit side of the ledger consists of the "diseconomies" or rigidities due to large scale, and the diseconomies or rigidities that may be associated with learning and experience. The effect of these countervailing rigidities may be to place large firms, or firms that have been in business a long time, at a competitive disadvantage compared to some smaller-scale, less-experienced, firms. In the realm of ideas that should vie for the allegiance of "practical men," the outcome is unclear. The intellectual case for smaller and newer firms is as strong as that for large, mature ones. Sometimes Goliath will win, other times David.

The Drawbacks of Size and Experience

Diseconomies of scale and of accumulated experience may be especially acute in an economic environment increasingly characterized by closer and multiple linkages between domestic and international markets. These linkages are accompanied by more rapid product and process innovation due to increasing speed and frequency of information transmission and reception (additions to the Internet have recently been running at a rate of 12 percent per month!), increased trade in goods, services and intellectual property (between 1986 and 1992 the volume of world trade grew at an annual rate more than twice as rapid as the rate of growth in world output), and increasing mobility of capital (as reflected by the increasingly close alignment of real interest rates in international markets).

In this rapidly changing environment, achievement of large scale and long experience may entail significant drawbacks—specifically, rigidities of scale and rigidities of learning.

First, consider the rigidities that often characterize large organizations because of the hierarchy, bureaucracy, standard operating procedures, and cumbersome administrative routines that they spawn. These characteristics may create a wedge between the lowered costs of acquiring information from *outside* a large organization—information about new production techniques, new products, new marketing and distribution methods resulting from the rapid pace of economic change and globalization mentioned earlier—and the higher costs of processing and utilizing information *inside* a large organization. The wedge between acquisition and utilization costs can lead to higher internal transaction costs, and slower response and reaction times in large organizations than in smaller ones.

Consequently, opportunities for developing new products and processes, or modifying old ones, may arise outside the large-scale firm, and even be observed by its members—products and processes that are closely related to, or substitutable for those of the large firm—without evoking an adequate or a timely response inside the firm. The limited and dilatory responses of General Motors in the 1980s, and of IBM, Toyota, Daimler-Benz, Sears Roebuck, and American Express in the 1990s, to changes and challenges in their respective industries, exemplify these countervailing tendencies. To be sure, there are counterexamples: General Electric, Alcoa, Sony, and the "Baby Bells" following the breakup of AT&T, have continued to be innovative and adaptive as well as large and experienced. That diseconomies of scale exist doesn't imply that they cannot be surmounted by large firms, nor that they will uniformly dominate the advantages of large size that were referred to earlier.

Diseconomies or rigidities of learning and experience arise in ways analogous to those associated with diseconomies of scale. Acquisition of experience, through a large volume of accumulated output over time, may immure the experienced firm by precisely what it has learned to do so well. Accumulated learning and experience may have a "lock-in" effect that induces lethargy and a failure to absorb and respond to product and process innovations that impend. These innovations may then displace or encroach upon the product line or the marketing style that the established firm has learned well and practiced long. Therefore, the experienced firm may be less accessible and receptive to information about innovations underway outside the firm, than are newer and less experienced firms.

Thus, the experienced firm may suffer from an insularity that drives a wedge between information that could be acquired from outside, and information that is actually acquired. The established and experienced firm may be placed at a disadvantage relative to newer and more nimble competitors. IBM's displacement by Apple in the personal computer business, and Intel's major gains over Hitachi in semiconductor dominance, are cases in point.

Rigidities of learning may be likened to the familiar left-brain, right-brain duality: overdevelopment of the left brain may result in an impediment to the stimulus and insight that the right brain can otherwise provide. Too much learning of one thing may be at the expense of reduced receptivity to learning other things.

So, the strong theoretical arguments for preferential industrial and trade policy confront equally powerful theoretical arguments against it. Large size and accumulated experience confer initial advantages, but may later entail offsetting disadvantages. This suggests there may be an optimum size—large, but not *too* large—and an optimum degree of experience—some, but not *too* much—that is conducive to strong competitive ability.

"Practical men" can be liberated from the thrall of the ideas underlying PITP by becoming aware that the supporting arguments are less convincing than they've been presumed to be, and that there are plausible arguments against them.

What About Japan?

Besides the captivating effect of some economists' theories about economies of scale and of experience, and the industrial policies and strategic trade policies these ideas ostensibly support, Japan's stellar economic performance is typically cited as a compelling example of the effectiveness of such policies and a demonstration of why the U.S. should adopt similar policies. Notwithstanding the fact that Japan's recent economic performance has been considerably less stellar than formerly—its negative real growth in 1992, and a barely positive one in 1993, are between 2 and 3 percentage points behind the corresponding rates in the U.S.— its economic accomplishments in the past two decades have demonstrated remarkably rapid growth, aggressive development of high technology industry, and a large and continuing current-account surplus with the United States and the rest of the world.

Some observers attribute this record to Japan's industrial and trade policies, orchestrated by the Ministry of International Trade and Industry (MITI), and encompassing various predatory Japanese business practices, "*Keiretsu*" industrial organizations, protection of the domestic market, discriminatory regulatory and contractual practices, and subsidized capital access for favored manufacturing industries. James Fallows invokes all of these to account for the rapid and profitable development of Japan's semiconductor industry in the 1980s (Fallows 1993), neglecting to mention, however, that the profits and the outlook of the principal movers in the industry—Hitachi, Toshiba, and NEC—have plummeted sharply in the 1990s. Moreover, even if MITI's trade and industrial policies were successful in semiconductors, its overall batting average looks much less impressive when account is taken of its efforts in other manufacturing industries—notably, steel, shipbuilding, and aircraft.

In any event, while MITI's record is at best mixed, Japan's remarkable economic accomplishments in the past two decades can be understood, and accounted for by simple explanations, without recourse to Japan's complex industrial and trade policies. The principle known as Occam's Razor suggests that simple explanations should be preferred to complex ones when both are available. Recourse to complexities should only be invoked when simple explanations prove inadequate.

The most compelling explanation for Japan's formidable economic accomplishments lies in four simple factors, some of which are likely to be transitory:

- *Investment*: Japan's annual rate of aggregate domestic investment averaged about 24 percent of its gross domestic product in the 1980s, compared with 15 to 16 percent in the United States.
- *Savings*: Japan's domestic savings averaged 28 percent of GNP in the same period, compared with only 13 to 14 percent in the U.S.
- *Labor*: Japan's work force is highly disciplined, trained, industrious, and literate.
- *Management*: Japanese managers are energetic, competent, and experienced, and they have learned—through international competition and the powerful dictates of the Japanese work ethic—to strive continually to improve product quality and cut production costs.

Japan's high domestic investment accounts for nearly all of the difference in average annual growth rates—about 2 or 3 percentage points—between Japan and the United States during the 1980s. Also, the investment difference largely explains Japan's strong performance in capital intensive sectors, like automobiles, consumer electronics, and semiconductors. Investment and savings, taken together, account for Japan's persistent trade surpluses (explained by the excess of Japan's savings over its investment), as well as the persistent trade deficits of the United States (explained by the excess of American investment over its savings). To be sure, public policies in Japan—specifically, tax policies—have provided strong incentives to boost both savings and investment: for example, by reducing the taxation of income that is saved rather than spent, by forgoing taxation of long-term capital gains, and by using a broader interpretation of what can be construed as research and development and thus can qualify for special tax advantages, than the interpretation that is allowed in the United States. These Japanese macroeconomic policies, which have strongly encouraged savings, long-term investment and R&D, contrast with ones in the United States that have not. And these Japanese policies have been pursued with a government sector that is about 20 percent smaller than that in the United States, as measured by the size of total government spending relative to GDP.

Together with the preceding factors, the quality of Japan's labor and of its management practices account for the relatively more rapid growth of Japanese productivity—until the past four or five years when U.S. labor productivity growth has equaled or exceeded that of Japan.

Nevertheless, after Japan recovers from its currently severe recession, the country's savings rate may fall somewhat as a result of rising consumer demand, and a population whose proportion of elderly people is increasing more rapidly than that of the United States and other industrialized countries. Japan's investment rate may also decrease due to tighter capital markets, and a reallocation of resources from the private to the public sector. As a result, its productivity growth will probably also decrease in the coming years.

In short, application of Occam's Razor suggests that the principal explanation for Japan's impressive economic accomplishments, and for its prominent position in the world economy, is quite independent of its industrial policy and its "strategic," neo-mercantilist trade practices.

This conclusion doesn't mean that U.S. negotiators, dealing bilaterally with the Japanese as well as multilaterally in GATT, should refrain from continued efforts to change Japan's atavistic policies and practices. On the contrary, the United States should seek to bring such liberalizing changes about, even though they would principally benefit Japanese consumers rather than American exporters (because the exporters of other countries would get some share of the increased trade with Japan that would result). It remains an unresolved question whether these changes are more likely to ensue through U.S. efforts to exert external pressure directly (*gaiatsu*) or instead through more indirect means, such as assisting Japanese consumers to exert pressure internally (*naiatsu*).

The Politics of Preferential Industrial
and Trade Policies in the United States

Even if the theoretical basis for PITP didn't suffer from the shortcomings discussed earlier, and even if the example of Japan provided clearer evidence in its support, the political realities of attempting to implement such preferential policies in the United States would make this an unpromising course to follow.

Strategic trade policy, or "industrial policy," or "managed trade" inevitably imply that some industrial or technological categories—semiconductors, automobiles, electronics, machine tools, pharmaceuticals, or rice—would be chosen for preferential treatment because they are considered "critical" for one reason or another. Responding to this incentive, "rational" firms and trade associations acting in the interest of their respective constituencies can be expected to allocate more time, attention, and resources to lobbying activities to obtain the potential preferment. Innovative and creative talent would be deployed either to develop persuasive reasons why particular technological or industrial categories should be interpreted so as to allow the interested parties to qualify for preferential treatment, or to argue for adding other categories because they are essential to complement and reinforce those already established. In a world of finite resources, these redeployments will be at the expense of allocating the corresponding resources toward more directly and economically productive pursuits. The outcome of such interest-group competition in the American political arena will reward the most successful political representations, rather than the most technologically promising firms. There is no particular reason for expecting these two domains to coincide. Even if it can be convincingly argued that computer chips are different from potato chips because the former generate positive "externalities," the case for preferential policies is unconvincing on political grounds. If such policies were put in place, a swarm of second and third-tier claimants will emerge with various degrees of persuasive arguments for their inclusion within the preferential safety net.

In sum, whatever the acknowledged shortcomings of the market and the merits of considering ways to remedy them, invoking preferential public policies toward this end entails the inevitable risk of other shortcomings that will accompany the remedial public policies. This is not to say that remedial public policies should not be considered. Rather, it is to add a note of caution lest attempts to rectify the shortcomings of the market lead to greater shortcomings of the attempted non-market remedies. Attempted therapies may be as bad as, or worse than, the maladies they seek to cure. The most promising industrial and trade policy for the United States is to persist in bringing the protracted Uruguay round of GATT to a successful conclusion, thereby promoting more open and competitive international markets for services and intellectual property, as well as commodities.

Summer 1994

4

Glib Rhetoric, Loose Thinking

Paul Krugman is one of the two most vocal, inventive, and widely known *enfants terribles* among the baby-boomer generation of economists. (The other is temporarily less vocal because of his position as a senior sub-cabinet official in the Clinton administration.) Mr. Krugman's *Pop Internationalism* (MIT Press) is a collection of thirteen essays, all but one previously published between 1991 and 1995. The exception is a thorough and deftly critical review of a 1993 book by Laura Tyson, *Who's Bashing Whom?*, which the *New York Review of Books* declined to publish because of the political incorrectness of Mr. Krugman's review. ("You're criticizing some very prestigious people," the editor told Mr. Krugman in rejecting his review—Ms. Tyson was at the time chairman of President Clinton's Council of Economic Advisors.)

Mr. Krugman defines "pop internationalism" as "glib rhetoric that appeals to those who want to sound sophisticated without engaging in hard thinking." Among the principal pop internationalists whose glib rhetoric and "intellectual laziness" the author demolishes are Lester Thurow, a former MIT colleague before Mr. Krugman moved to Stanford a couple of years ago, Robert Reich, currently the secretary of labor, James Fallows, a writer for *The Atlantic Monthly*, and Robert Kuttner at *The American Prospect*.

Mr. Krugman's dispositive treatment of these pop internationalists exposes their theoretical as well as empirical errors. Among the principal ones are the following:

• The analogy that pop internationalists typically draw between competition among firms and competition among countries is based on a fundamental mistake: when firms compete with one another, there are both losses and gains; the outcome is zero-sum. By contrast, trade competition between countries results in gains from trade. International trade is a positive-sum process, although the distribution of the gains between the parties can be quite asymmetrical.

• Economic growth in third world countries, leading to their expanded role in the global economy, generally has positive, rather than adverse, effects on the first world. Mistakenly, pop internationalists see third world growth as having negative impacts on the U.S. and other developed countries.

• Whereas pop internationalist rhetoric typically asserts that the rate of growth in real wages in the United States has been adversely affected by competition from low-wage countries, Mr. Krugman shows that in fact the slow growth in real wages in the U.S. has occurred "almost entirely for domestic reasons," not international ones.

• Mr. Krugman also calculates that, were the U.S. to adopt a "strategic trade policy"—a staple of pop internationalist rhetoric—the results would have negligible effects on the U.S. economy, raising it by only 1/15th of 1 percent of the U.S. GDP. And this would ensue only under the theoretically most favorable assumptions. Under more realistic ones, the results would probably be growth inhibiting.

Mr. Krugman's devastating criticism of the pop internationalists places him in an awkward position because he himself provided the intellectual underpinnings for the pop internationalist views that he now dismantles. In the 1980s, when Krugman was a professor at MIT, he played a central role in developing the so-called "new trade theory." This theory reinvented eighteenth-century mercantilism, updating it with the modern trappings of market failures, potential gains from economies of scale, economies of learning, and the creation of externalities. The theory held out the prospect that the whole economy would benefit from astute policy engineering in the form of preferential treatment of key, high-tech industries.

What the new trade theory overlooked, of course, was the consequential risks of *non*market failure. Attempts by government to remedy the market's shortcomings often lead to distortions and misallocations that exceed the shortcomings of the market.

It was a short and predictable leap from the theoretical possibility, originally developed by Mr. Krugman and others, to the pop internationalism that he now understandably and effectively criticizes. Mr. Krugman is not unaware of "a certain irony" in the fact that he is now "playing the role of defender of civilized economics against the intellectual barbarians"—a nice example of the "engineer hoist with his own petard!"

May 1996

5

Taxes, Trade, and Growth

After the party conventions conclude in August, it can be expected, or at least hoped, that the presidential campaigns will turn to substantive issues like economic growth, employment, wages, taxes, and trade. If and when this occurs, the ensuing debate should address one of the most basic, as well as most important, relationships in economics: that between the savings-investment balance, on the one hand, and the trade balance (or, more accurately, the current account balance), on the other. To the extent that domestic savings fall short of domestic investment, the economy must import more than it exports. So, if the savings-investment balance is negative, then the economy's trade balance will also be negative.

The importance of this relationship transcends that of the balance between federal government expenditures and revenues—that is, the budget deficit. The budget deficit is one among several factors influencing the savings-investment balance. Other factors include the absolute amount of government spending (quite apart from the size of the budget deficit itself), tax and regulatory incentives to save and invest, monetary policy, and demographics.

The singular importance of the balance between domestic savings and domestic investment is due to several of its consequences, including the link it provides between the domestic and international economies. This balance maps directly into changes in American holdings of assets abroad, and to changes in assets held in the United States by other governments, as well as by corporate and individual entities domiciled in other countries. Over time, the savings-investment balance determines whether the American economy earns more in interest and dividends from its foreign holdings than it pays to other economies on their holdings in the United States. This, in turn, determines whether the gross *national* product is larger or smaller than the gross *domestic* product. (The difference be-

27

tween GNP and GDP is net income received from, or paid to, the rest of the world: GNP is less than GDP when we pay more to the rest of the world than the income we receive from it, and vice versa.)

Furthermore, the savings-investment balance significantly affects the growth of employment and wages, as well as the economy's overall rate of growth. Boosting domestic savings and investment—and, in particular, boosting savings by more than investment—is also of central importance for reversing the perennial U.S. pattern of importing capital from abroad to finance the excess of U.S. imports over its exports.

For the past decade, the U.S. has experienced a shortfall of gross domestic savings compared to gross domestic investment. This perennial shortfall has varied between one and two percent of the GDP, averaging about 100 billion dollars annually from 1985 through 1995. This savings shortfall is reflected by the excess of U.S. imports of goods and services over our exports. As a consequence of the cumulative shortfall in annual savings, about 18 percent (about $750 billion) of total U.S. public debt is held abroad.

To improve the performance of the American economy, policies should be pursued that will increase both investment and savings, but will increase savings by more than the increase in investment—thereby, reducing or reversing the savings shortfall referred to earlier. Accomplishing this goal would mean that the current account deficit of the past decade would be replaced by a current account surplus, that U.S. exports would increase by more than increases in imports, that additional and relatively high-paying jobs would be generated (because wages in exporting industries are about 15 to 18 percent above average wages), and that U.S. economic growth would rise. As a consequence, U.S. import of capital would be reversed and the burden of servicing foreign-held debt would be eased. Instead, U.S. exports of capital would result in our receiving net income from abroad, rather than incurring net servicing obligations to other countries.

So much for *what* needs to be done and *why*. The next question is *how* can this be done—that is, how can investment and savings be raised, while raising savings more than investment? Several options are worth considering—their respective economic merits may be uncorrelated, or even negatively correlated, with their political merits and political feasibility. One option would be a straight across-the-board reduction in marginal tax rates, perhaps by 5 percent, 5 percent, and 3 percent, corresponding to the three presently graduated marginal tax rates. The expanded tax base that such a change in marginal rates would create is likely to minimize the resulting reductions in revenue yields, and perhaps to avoid such reductions entirely.

A second option would focus more directly on incentives to save—for example, by eliminating taxation of interest and dividend income, and expanding the tax-deductibility of 401 (k) contributions and IRAs (for example, to include nonworking spouses as proposed in a bi-partisan bill presently under consideration in Congress).

A third option is to move gradually toward an equitably graduated consumption-based tax structure with exemptions and lower rates applying to smaller consumption outlays, and a higher rate applying to larger consumption outlays.

Some worry—not without reason—that a consumption-type system might generate a deluge of revenues, thereby tempting future administrations and Congresses to increase spending. To ease this concern, a consumption-based system might be accompanied by automatic caps that would be triggered if revenues exceeded the standard 19 to 20 percent of GDP typically represented by federal government revenues over the past two decades.

Pursuing one or more of these options, while maintaining a suitably prudent set of monetary policies, will improve the economy's performance by raising annual growth—perhaps by 0.5 percent or 1.0 percent—from, say, 2.5 percent to 3.0 percent or 3.5 percent, thereby adding $35 to 70 billion annually to GDP.

August 1996

6

Global Competition for Long-Term Capital: Who Will Win?

Rising Demands for Long-Term Capital

If East Asia, with a population of about 1.8 billion, continues its extraordinarily high rate of growth through the 1990s and beyond; if South Asia, with a population of 1.2 billion, ratchets up its recent growth toward that of East Asia; if Latin America, with a population of 450 million, resumes its high growth of the late 1980s and early 1990s; and if Eastern Europe, Russia, Ukraine, and the Central Asian Republics, with a combined population of about 400 million, succeed in economic liberalization that moves them to a path of sustained economic growth, their combined demand for long-term capital investment will be enormous. Clearly, the bulk of these demands will have to be met from internal sources. Yet, there will be a large residual constituting an increasing demand for long-term capital from the international capital market.

So, the question arises where will the long-term capital come from, and who will be the winners and the losers in the competition for it?

The answer to the first question is that, in general, the OECD developed countries, in Western Europe, the United States, Japan, Australia, and New Zealand, with a combined population of about 650 million, will be the principal sources of global savings and of long-term capital. Yet, their supply of capital will be limited by their own domestic demands for new investment in their private sectors, by their public infrastructure demands, and by their commitments to the social welfare programs their political structures maintain. As a consequence, the bulk of the long-term capital demands of the developing regions will have to be provided from their own sources of domestic savings. This has been an abiding

31

characteristic of all prior development experience, and will continue to be the case in the future.

However, there will be a residual representing the difference between long-term capital demands in the previously mentioned developing regions, and their domestic savings; and this residual will be reflected by demands in the global capital market. Consequently, competition for long-term capital flows in that market will be intense in the years ahead.

Before considering the determinants of future capital flows, the next section of this paper briefly describes the different types of long-term capital flows, and the record of prior flows in the period from 1985 to 1993.

Types of Long-Term Capital Flows and Prior Flows, 1985–1993

Long-term capital flows are composed of five principal types shown in figure 6.1 below:

FIGURE 6.1
Types of Long-Term Capital Flows

- Foreign direct investment
- Portfolio equity   } "voluntary"
- LT private non-guaranteed debt
- LT public and publicly guaranteed debt
- Grants

As indicated in figure 6.1, the first three types are "voluntary"—that is, they flow as a result of business, rather than government, decisions and are motivated principally by market and profit considerations. Foreign direct investment is defined as acquisition of 10 percent or more of the assets of a business entity abroad, and typically takes the form of tangible, real-property, "bricks and mortar" investment. Portfolio equity investment represents asset acquisitions that are less than the 10 percent equity threshold. Long-term private nonguaranteed debt consists of commercial loans of more than one-year's maturity.

Voluntary capital—that is, the first three types shown in figure 6.1—is heavily dependent upon the policy and politics of host governments, including their overall prospects for political stability, which, of course,

TABLE 6.1
Long-Term Net Capital Inflows[1]—1985–1993
(in billions of current dollars)

	1985–1989 (1)	Annual Average (2)	1990–1993 (3)	Annual Average (4)	(4/2)
FDI	97.0	19.2	186.1	46.5	2.4
Portfolio equity	30.6[2]	7.6[2]	82.8	20.1	2.7
Long-term private non-guaranteed debt	–25.4	–5.1	71.0	17.7	4.5[3]
Long-term public and publicly guaranteed debt	394.0	78.9	183.2	45.8	.58
Grants	107.2	21.4	152.3	38.1	1.8
Totals	603.4	122.1	675.4	168.2	1.4

Sources: World Bank *Debt Tables*, IMF *Balance of Payments Yearbook*, OECD, and BIS.

Notes: 1. Net flows *to* East Asia and Pacific, Europe and Central Asia, Latin America, Middle East, South Asia, Sub-Saharan Africa, *from* OECD.
2. 1986–1989
3. Calculated from absolute values.

affect the reliability of market and profit calculations. By contrast, public and publicly guaranteed debt, as well as grants, depend on the policies, priorities and preferences of donor governments and international agencies. Lending by the Export-Import Bank, OPIC guaranteed debt, and grants from the Agency for International Development, as well as its counterpart agencies in the other OECD countries, are principally motivated by policy considerations that differ from the commerical considerations motivating the three voluntary types of capital flows.

Table 6.1 shows the distribution of long-term capital inflows across the five principal types shown in figure 6.1, from 1985 through 1993, in billions of current dollars.

As table 6.1 indicates, in the last part of the 1980s net long-term capital flows were dominated by public debt, publicly guaranteed debt, and grants, amounting to over $500 billion during the 1985-1989 period, while the "voluntary" forms of capital flows amounted to less than $100 billion (after allowance for the net repayment of previously accumulated private, non-guaranteed debt, by the capital importing, countries). In the first four years of the 1990s, by contrast with the earlier period, the

TABLE 6.2
Long-Term Capital Growth Rates[1]
Growth Rates (%)—1985–1993

	1985	1993	Compound Growth Rate
	(billions of current dollars)		(%/yr)
FDI	14.1	68.8	19
Portfolio equity	22.3[2]	81.1	20
Long-term private nonguaranteed debt	–3.6	23.2	25[3]
Long-term public and publicly guaranteed debt	88.1	65.7	–.3
Grants	15.5	37.6	10
Totals	136.4	276.4	8

Sources: World Bank *Debt Tables*, IMF *Balance of Payments Yearbook*, OECD, and BIS.

Notes: 1. Net flows *to* East Asia-Pacific, Europe/Central Asia, Latin America, Middle East, South Asia, Sub-Saharan Africa, *from* OECD.
2. 1987 figure
3. Calculated from absolute values.

voluntary sources of capital—especially foreign direct investment—substantially increased. The combination of foreign direct investment, portfolio equity, and long-term private nonguaranteed debt slightly exceeded the volume of publicly provided capital ($340 billion for the voluntary types of capital flows versus $336 billion for the publicly-provided debts and grants).

Table 6.2 shows the annual compound growth rates of the five different types of long-term capital flows between 1985 and 1993. Whereas total long-term capital flows increased at an annual rate of 8 percent (in current dollars), the three voluntary sources of long-term capital flows increased at annual compound rates between 19 percent and 25 percent, while long-term public and publicly guaranteed debt, and grants taken together show no change during the 1985 through 1993 period.

The preceding tables tell a dramatic story that can be summarized in the following principal points:

1. From 1985 to 1993, average annual flows of long-term capital increased by 40 percent (recalling, again, that these figures are in current dollars and would be reduced by a third if the data were expressed in constant dollars).

2. During this period, the composition of long-term capital flows changed dramatically. "Voluntary" flows increased fivefold, while annual government and multilateral sources—that is government grants, and guaranteed debt—were unchanged.

3. Within these totals, foreign direct investment, portfolio equity investment, and private nonguaranteed debt experienced double-digit growth rates. In contrast, aggregate public flows experienced a negative annual growth rate, although the grant proportion of the total increased modestly.

4. Thus, long-term capital flows in the aggregate are increasingly dominated by private flows which comprised 63 percent of the total in 1993, compared with 24 percent in 1985.

Recipients of Long-Term Capital Flows

Among the developing, non-OECD regions, the largest recipient of the flows summarized in figure 6.1 and the previous two tables were in the Asia-Pacific region, reflecting, as well as contributing to that region's impressive—double digit or high-single digit GDP growth rates (excepting that of Japan which, in the past four years, has hovered around 1 percent per annum). Between 1985 and 1993, foreign direct investment in the Asia-Pacific region increased sevenfold from $6 billion in 1985 to over $45 billion in 1993. The region experienced still larger relative increases in portfolio equity and long-term nonguaranteed debt flows.

From 1985 through the start of 1994, net global long-term capital flows totaled $1.3 trillion of which 60 percent went to the Asia-Pacific region, another 15 percent was destined for Latin America, 10 percent to South Asia, with smaller amounts going to the Middle East, eastern Europe, and still smaller amounts to sub-Saharan Africa.

Determinants of Future Long-Term Capital Flows

The destinations of future long-term capital flows from the wealthier OECD countries will depend on three factors: prior capital flows, expected future economic growth, and the economic, political, legal, and security environment of prospective recipient countries. Having already summarized the pattern of prior capital flows, we turn to consider briefly the two other factors.

Generally, the pattern and experience associated with prior capital flows will have a significantly positive influence on the magnitudes and patterns of future flows. The reason is that the experience and the precedents connected with prior capital flows typically entail a learning process that adds to the available fund of information about future investment. Answering the question of whether and how much to invest in country "A" rather than country "B,"may be facilitated by prior experience in investing in either or both. The effect of this learning and information acquisition is to lower transactions costs for future investors, both FDI and portfolio equity investors.

To be sure, a countervailing influence may also operate: namely, diminishing marginal returns for further capital flows. In some cases, the best investment opportunities may be skimmed by the first capital flows, so that the next phase of investment opportunities may be less appealing. In most cases, however, I would expect that the positive benefits from previously accumulated experience and learning, reflected by prior capital flows, will have a stronger effect in inducing further capital flows, than the negative effect of diminishing marginal returns in reducing those flows.

The second major influence on future capital flows is the expectations of future economic growth associated with individual countrries and sectors within them. Regions where economies remain strong, and business is expected to expand along with the growth of their internal markets, will tend to attract foreign investors looking for expanded sales and profits. Conversely, areas where growth rates are flat or diminishing are less likely to attract investment.

As shown in table 6.3, the World Bank has made preliminary estimates of annual GDP growth in the Lower and Middle Income Countries (LMIC) for the 1995–2004 decade.

Growth in the Asia-Pacific region is estimated to be highest (7.6 percent), followed by South Asia (6.9 percent), Latin America (6 percent), with somewhat lower rates for eastern Europe, Russia., the Central Asian Republics of the former Soviet Union, the Middle East and sub-Saharan Africa.

For the LMIC group, the World Bank estimates that aggregate annual growth for the 1995-2004 period will be 6.5 percent. Within these regions, the Bank forecasts China's annual growth as the highest at 8.5 percent per annum, followed by India's 7.1 percent.

As is also shown in table 6.3, RAND has made independent estimates that place China's and India's growth rates somewhat lower than the optimistic estimates of the World Bank, at 4.9 percent and 5.5 percent,

TABLE 6.3
Expected Economic Growth

Expected Economic Growth (%/yr)	
• World Bank estimates, 1995–2004	
– all "LMI" countries	6.5%
– Asia-Pacific (China: 8.5)	7.6
– South Asia (India: 7.1)	6.9
– Latin America	6.0
– EE & FSU	4.0
• RAND estimates:	
– China	4.9
– Indonesia	5.1
– India	5.5
– Korea	7.9

respectively. The RAND estimates also place Indonesia's and Korea's respective growth rates over this period at 5.1 percent and 7.9 percent, respectively.[1]

In sum, if buoyant growth in the LMI regions in fact materializes, it will provide a powerful attraction for the three types of voluntary long-term capital inflows. Reflecting this connection between expected economic growth and capital inflows, the World Bank has made buoyant estimates of future foreign direct investment. The Bank has forecasted a doubling of annual flows between 1995 ($61 billion) and 2004 ($122 billion), with two-thirds of these totals expected to flow to the Asia-Pacific region (of which China would receive nearly 60 percent), and only 5 percent to India. Another 15 to 20 percent of the total FDI estimate is forecast by the Bank to flow to Latin America. In all probability, the potential flows of portfolio equity investment would be at least as large as those associated with foreign direct investment.

Finally, the pattern of future capital flows will be increasingly dependent on the broad investment climate—that is, the economic, political, legal, and security environment—prevailing and impending in the LMI countries. The voluntary types of capital flows, that we expect to become increasingly important, are likely to be especially responsive to host-country policies—particularly to macroeconomic policies affecting inflation, tax structure, and currency convertibility, as well as the predictability of property rights and the rule of law, regulatory policies, and the general outlook for political stability. Within this matrix of broad environmental influences, the enforceability of contractual obligations by local and central governments will be another important conditioning influence. In some countries, such as China, the role of the military establishment, and its interaction with the civil economy, may either enhance or erode political stability, with corresponding effects on conditions and incentives for capital inflows.

Concluding Observations

Developing countries that hope to attract foreign capital to help finance their economic growth will face international markets in which the supply of capital from the wealthier nations is likely to be constrained by their own capital demands, and by their continued high-level of public spending on social programs. Consequently, these developing LMIC regions will have to rely predominantly on domestic savings to finance their economic growth. This is not unusual—it has been the pattern of development financing that has prevailed in the past in Western Europe, the United States and Japan.

So, international capital markets will be intensely competitive. In this ensuing competition for scarce long-term capital, the winners will be those that are successful in sustaining high levels of economic growth, and those whose economic, legal, and regulatory policies meet the concerns of foreign investors, and engage the "animal spirits" that often motivate them.

December 1995

Note

1. Charles Wolf, Jr., K.C. Yeh, et al., *Long-Term Economic and Military Trends, 1994–2015,* RAND, MR-627, 1995.

7

What's Behind the Weak Dollar?

The dollar's depreciation between end-of-year 1993 and 1994—11 percent relative to the Japanese yen, 9 percent relative to the German mark, and 6 percent relative to the British pound—is one of those puzzling paradoxes that not infrequently occur in the marketplace. While the dollar depreciated, the U.S. economy's performance continued to be much stronger and more vigorous than that of the European and Japanese economies whose currencies appreciated. In comparison with those economies, U.S. GDP growth has been rapid, unemployment has decreased, productivity and corporate profits have risen, prices have been stable, and the dollar's relative purchasing power has increased.

These circumstances might have led one to expect the dollar's exchange value to rise, rather than fall. Indeed, one acknowledged expert in the complexities of international finance, George Soros, reportedly lost about $1 billion betting that this would happen!

The explanation usually offered is the U.S. current account deficit: the excess of U.S. outlays for imports of goods and services over receipts from exports thereof. While this is surely a part of the explanation, by itself it is insufficient. The larger part lies in the size and composition of U.S. capital *exports*.

The usual explanation that emphasizes the current account deficit argues that the payments required to cover it increase the supply of dollars in foreign exchange markets, thereby depressing the dollar's exchange value. But this deficit is relatively small—about $80 billion in 1993, and probably about $100 billion in 1994—less than 1.5 percent of the U.S. GDP. Consequently, one might have expected that foreign investors, responding to the strongly favorable signs in the U.S. economy, would have aggressively sought out assets in the U.S. in amounts at least equivalent to the current account deficit, thereby sustaining or even bidding up the dollar's exchange value.

What is overlooked by the current account deficit as an explanation for the dollar's decline is the unprecedented phenomenon that underlies the dollar's depreciation: The U.S. has been the world's largest capital *exporter* at the same time as it has been the world's largest capital *importer*!

In 1993, U.S. capital exports were the largest of any country, rising to $148 billion, principally due to a surge of U.S. investments in foreign equities by mutual funds, pension funds, and individuals (totaling $120 billion), as well as U.S. direct investment abroad. For the first half of 1994, the corresponding figures are $50 billion for total U.S. capital outflows, of which $37 billion represents increased holdings of foreign securities, and $33 billion is direct investment abroad. (Reductions by U.S. banks in their claims on foreign banks, accounts for most of the difference between total outflows in the first half of 1994, $50 billion, and the sum of portfolio and direct investment, $70 billion.)

U.S. capital imports have also been the world's largest, necessarily exceeding the magnitude of our capital exports by an amount sufficient to provide financing for the current account deficit. In 1993, total capital inflow into the United States reached $231 billion. Of this amount, over 40 percent represented increased holdings by foreign governments and individuals of U.S. government assets, with the remainder divided among foreign direct investment in the U.S., bank loans, and foreign investment in U.S. equities and bonds. For the first half of 1994 the corresponding figure for total capital inflow into the United States is $137 billion, of which about $20 billion consisted of increased foreign government holdings of U.S. assets, $60 billion represented loans to U.S. banks, and the remainder was divided among direct investment and increased holdings of U.S. securities.

How does a combination of the large U.S. capital exports and the still larger volume of capital imports bring about depreciation of the dollar?

Underlying the surge of U.S. portfolio investment abroad has been the proliferation and expansion of international, and "emerging market" global equity, funds. This surge is driven by the assessments of portfolio managers who tend to be less concerned with exchange-rate risks than with certain other, still more important considerations: the outlook for aggregate and sectoral growth in specific foreign countries; the competitive strength of specific foreign firms; the domestic, regional, and global market shares that these firms can acquire; their dividend policies and management capabilities; and the increased interest of U.S. mutual fund shareholders in risk diversification through investment in markets outside the U.S. These major movers of U.S. capital outflow have been sufficiently bullish about buying into foreign holdings to be willing to pay a higher dollar price for foreign exchange.

On the other hand, a larger share of capital imports into the United States represents foreign bank loans to U.S. banks, rather than equity investments. (One of the reasons accounting for the relatively small share of foreign equity investment in total U.S. capital imports is that U.S. tax withholding on earnings from such investments reduces the incentives of foreign investors and portfolio managers to buy U.S. equities.) These bank I.O.U.s tend to be responsive to changes in interest rates, and are more passive with respect to changes in exchange rates. They tend, therefore, not to have a major effect on exchange rates.

Thus, depreciation of the U.S. dollar is affected by the *composition,* as well as the size, of U.S. capital exports and capital imports. The net impact on the dollar's exchange rate is greater per dollar of capital exports than per dollar of capital imports because much of the capital exports are governed by U.S. investment portfolio managers who focus principally on considerations other than exchange rates in making their investment choices.

On this reasoning, the dollar might continue to depreciate even if the U.S. current account deficit diminishes, because U.S. portfolio and direct investment abroad might continue to be large. However, to the extent that the most lucrative niches in foreign equity markets have already been, or soon will be, filled, and the next-best equities are less attractive, U.S. capital exports will recede and the dollar's value will appreciate.

To assess whether the dollar's foreign exchange value is more likely to rise or fall, the place to look is the capital account, rather than only the current account. The outcome for the value of the dollar will depend on what happens to U.S. portfolio and direct investment abroad rather than what happens to the current account deficit.

February 1995

8

Who Really Needs a Country Anymore?

Exaggeration sometimes helps to make a valid point. Kenichi Ohmae does both in *The End of the Nation State: The Rise of Regional Economies* (Free Press). The valid and important point is that *information* forges powerful linkages among *investment, industry,* and *individual consumers*, and that these linkages transcend national borders, thereby eclipsing and rendering "dysfunctional" the nation state.

There is little question about the potent and pervasive influence of these "4-I's"—sometimes Mr. Ohmae refers to them, equivalently, as the "4-forces" of "communication, corporations, capital, and consumers." Nevertheless, it is an exaggeration to equate this with the "end" of the nation state. National governments retain powerful instruments that can be used for good (sometimes) or ill (not infrequently): notably, military forces, national or local police power, and the power to make macroeconomic fiscal and monetary policies and to establish legal infrastructures covering property rights, contract enforcement, and dispute resolution. These instruments, in turn, significantly affect the operations of Mr. Ohmae's "4-I's" or "4-forces," in a global economy that is, as he repeatedly and justifiably reminds us, increasingly becoming "borderless."

Many of the core ideas elaborated here by Mr. Ohmae—the borderless world, the information-driven global linkages among companies, interest groups, and individuals in different regions and countries, and the eclipse of the nation state—are less novel but no less valid or significant than they were when he originally advanced them in previous books and articles.

In his new book, Mr. Ohmae develops several new themes, while repeating and elaborating the more familiar ones. One of the new themes is an effective rebuttal of the "clash-of-civilizations" hypothesis propounded by Professor Samuel Huntington of Harvard several years ago. Huntington argued that civilizations and cultures—Judaeo-Christian, Sinitic,

Japanese, Islamic, Hindu—would be the dominant as well as divisive influences in international affairs in the coming years. Mr. Ohmae's effective rebuttal argues instead that information-driven linkages will exert a stronger countervailing "centripetal" force transcending these cultures as well as the nation states.

Mr. Ohmae also advances the notion that, in place of feckless nation states, the effective new "natural economic zones" are "regional states" that become synergistically joined through their shared economic and technological interests, innovations, and economic activities. His designated "region states" include Baden-Wurtemberg, Wales, San Diego/Tijuana, Hong Kong/Southern China, the Silicon Valley/Bay Area in California, the Growth Triangle of Singapore, Johore and the neighboring Riau Islands, the Research Triangle Park in North Carolina, Tokyo and its outlying areas, Osaka and the Kansai region, as well as others. This thesis, which recalls Michael Porter's idea of economic "clusters" and, from an earlier day, Alfred Marshall's notion of "agglomerative" economies, is at least partly weakened by some of the arguments advanced by Ohmae himself. In the world of the 4-I's and 4-forces, companies can and do forge alliances and find partners that are often as remote from the specified "regional states" as they are from national ones. In a "borderless world," the reach may extend beyond regional as well as beyond national states. For example, the Sumitomo Bank in Tokyo reached to the Ford Motor Company in Michigan to help in restructuring Mazda in Japan, and U.S. money managers in New York and California are partnering with Russian, Indian, and Korean financial institutions to establish mutual funds in those countries.

Interestingly, but not surprisingly, Ohmae's view of Japan's own socio-cultural-economic system contrasts sharply with that of the "revisionist" school of Japanologists in the United States. Whereas the revisionists see Japan's system as completely static, and controlled by the triangular elite of the government bureaucracy, big business, and compliant political parties, Ohmae sees Japan's increasingly computerized society and its "Nintendo kids" as embarked on "an entirely new way of thinking" in which "nothing need be accepted as an unalterable *fait accompli*." In Mr. Ohmae's view, "the link among generations has been broken; a new link with those sharing similar experiences has been forged."

Mr. Ohmae, a senior partner and managing director of McKinsey and Company's Tokyo office for the past two decades, recently resigned from that position to become a candidate (unfortunately, an unsuccessful one) for mayor of Tokyo. Notwithstanding this initial setback, it is to be hoped that he, in association with like-minded colleagues, will become an influential voice in Japanese politics in the future.

July 1995

9

Why Asia Will Matter More Than Europe

Viewed from a Washington, D.C. perspective, Europe and the Atlantic generally seem closer, more accessible, and more important than Asia and the Pacific. Deep and abiding linkages of culture, history, politics, and economics underlie this European orientation of much U.S. policymaking and many policymakers. But this perspective is anachronistic. If "economic security" policy is to be at least equal in importance to "national security" policy, as the Clinton administration intends, and if economic strength in the 1990s is considered no less significant than military strength, as much of the newly conventional thinking on foreign policy asserts, then U.S. policymakers should devote more attention to the Asia Pacific (AP) region in the coming years, even if this means less devoted to Europe.

This change in regional priorities suggests that President Clinton's Departments of State and Commerce, under Secretaries Warren Christopher and Ronald Brown, respectively, and the U.S. Trade Representative Mickey Kantor, should post their best and brightest to work in or on the AP region. Furthermore, federal government agencies should emulate the efforts of many state governments in devoting more of their trade and investment promotion efforts to the AP region, while state governments should continue and reinforce their own efforts as well. And the U.S. Information Agency's Voice of America programming, cultural activities, and foreign leaders' travel grants should place relatively more emphasis on the AP region and AP audiences. Finally, because *economic* security and *national* security policies are likely to be closely related in the AP region, Defense Secretary Les Aspin should be intimately involved in these reorientation efforts.

There are impressive, well-known, but often forgotten reasons that warrant such a shift in the regional emphasis of U.S. policy.

The AP region in the 1990s will encompass the world's most rapidly growing countries. Within this region, China is likely to be the fastest growing economy with an annual growth rate of about 6 percent, while Japan is likely to have the slowest growth in the region (between 2 and 2.5 percent annually), except perhaps for that of the Philippines. In between, but probably much closer to China's growth rate than to Japan's will be the other AP economies—Taiwan, Hong Kong (becoming part of China in 1997), Indonesia, Thailand, Singapore, Malaysia, and Korea—assuming that Korea's management of eventual reunification with the North is accomplished peacefully and successfully.

Together the gross national products of the AP economies account for more than 20 percent of the global product—slightly less than the corresponding shares of the United States (23 percent) and the European Community (28 percent). Within the AP region, China's GNP (which, according to RAND analysis, is about three-times as large as the estimate usually cited by the World Bank and other international agencies) will probably exceed that of Japan before the end of the 1990s. The AP share of the global product will increase appreciably in the coming years because the region's growth rate will be twice that of the two other principal economic regions—the European Community and the North American Free Trade Area.

The volume of AP foreign trade is already substantial by global standards—currently its share in global trade is about 22 percent compared to 18 percent for the U.S., Canada, and Mexico, and 38 percent for the EC (more than half of which is intra-European trade)—and the AP trade share can be expected to increase dramatically in the coming decade. The reason is that imports usually are highly responsive to income growth. Since the AP region's growth will be the world's highest, trade and investment access to its rapidly expanding markets will be among the world economy's principal engines of growth. Consequently, such access—or impediments to it—will increasingly dominate the world's economic agenda during the next decade.

In its dealings with the Asia-Pacific economies, the U.S. will confront large issues that can be lucrative or costly depending on how they are resolved. They will probably be at least as difficult as those that have afflicted the nearly concluded six-year negotiations of the Uruguay Round of the General Agreement on Tariffs and Trade (GATT). The issues relating to soybeans and oilseeds, that have entailed so much acrimony in

U.S. relations with France, are relatively "small potatoes" by comparison with those that will arise in economic relations with the AP region in the coming decade.

U.S. economic relations with the AP countries will confront pervasive as well as subtle forms of neo-mercantilist policies—not less formidable than those that have occupied center stage in the GATT arena and in negotiations between the U.S. and the EC. In addition to the use of subsidies to sustain and encourage high-cost agricultural production—the standard pattern of protectionism in Europe—the AP countries practice dual-pricing policies (for example, domestic prices of Japanese and Chinese consumer goods are substantially higher than the corresponding dollar prices of the same products typically charged in foreign markets by Japanese and Chinese producers). Also, the AP countries often use tax rebates to encourage exports, tax surcharges to discourage imports, arbitrary customs classifications, as well as restrictions or outright exclusion of certain categories of services or commodity imports (for example, foreign-made cars in Korea), and foreign investments in certain economic sectors.

Although all of these issues have arisen in prior U.S. trade negotiations with Europe and in GATT, their frequency and prominence are likely to grow as their principal venue shifts from Europe to the AP region. Within the AP region, U.S. relations with China will be of growing importance, as well as complicated by two special considerations. First, during 1993, it is likely that China will be admitted to GATT. Because GATT members accord most-favored-nation (MFN) status reciprocally and automatically to other members, the U.S. will be hard pressed to deny this status to China once it becomes a member of GATT. As a result, leverage on China's human rights behavior, that the U.S. has exercised by its annual consideration of whether or not to grant China MFN access to the U.S. market, will be lost, or at least weakened.

Second, China's rapid overall economic growth has been and is likely to continue to be accompanied by substantial increases in its military spending, force modernization, and purchases as well as sales of weapons and military technology. Indeed, China is the only major power that is still increasing its military spending substantially. Whether and how this enhanced military strength will be used may pose serious problems in a world that increasingly adheres to the view that military strength is decreasing in importance relative to economic strength.

In the coming decade the AP region as a whole will require more of the time and attention of U.S. policymakers and, within the region, China is likely to warrant increasing emphasis.

January 1993

10

Clintonomics *versus* Reaganomics

President Clinton's State of the Union message to the Congress on February 17, 1993 defined a broad economic agenda for the nation, as President Reagan had done twelve years earlier. Like the debate that ensued over Reaganomics, the impending debate over Clintonomics will deal as much with politics as with economics. But in other respects, the character of the Clintonomics debate will be strikingly different.

During the early Reagan years, the economic debate was principally between those *inside* the administration, or very closely linked to it—Martin Anderson, Robert Mundell, Robert Bartley, Jack Kemp, and Jude Wanniski—and those *outside*—including many mainline economists in academia. For the most part, it was also a debate between those *inside* the Clinton administration than between them and those outside, including the Republicans. Moreover, the debate's agenda will be notably different.

The Reaganomics debate of the 1980s focused on monetary policy and supply-side economics. (The "Laffer-curve" argument—that reducing tax *rates* might result in increasing tax *revenues*—was a component of supply-side economics.) Protagonists of Reaganomics asserted that both corrective monetary policy and new supply-side policies were essential and, moreover, that the neglect of supply-sideism was a yawning gap in standard economics. The response of the standard economists was that monetary policy was unreliable and that supply-sideism and Lafferism, while admittedly novel, were just plain wrong! (On the issue of novelty, both sides of the debate erred: these ideas had been advanced in detail decades earlier by Joseph Schumpeter, in a neglected monograph on the *Crisis of the Tax State*.)

The new debate over Clintonomics focuses on fiscal policy, rather than monetary policy, pitting fiscal "activists" against fiscal "conserva-

51

tives" within the Clinton entourage. Notwithstanding their differences, the contending sides agree on two core propositions that set them apart from the protagonists of Reaganomics: that government (especially the federal government) should play a more active role in guiding the economy, and that defense spending should be cut by more than the 20 percent reduction already planned over the next four years by the Bush administration. Thereafter, the two sides within the Clinton administration diverge sharply.

The "activists" consist of two groups: old fashioned Keynesians (like Nobel laureates, Robert Solow and James Tobin), who advocate a fiscal stimulus to the economy through increased government spending to boost aggregate demand, employment, and industrial capacity utilization; and the program activists, who are less concerned with aggregate spending than with increasing outlays on particular programs and sectors that they favor—for example, "infrastructure," health insurance for the uninsured, housing, education and training, environmental protection, community development, and advanced technologies. This group includes the corresponding cabinet heads—Donna Shalala, Robert Reich, Federico Pena, Henry Cisneros, Carol Browner—and Laura Tyson in the Council of Economic Advisors. They may differ with one another over program priorities, but can be expected to make common cause with the Keynesian activists in promoting what they believe is needed to reduce one or another aspect of the nation's so-called "investment deficit." However, the Keynesians' influence will continue to be weakened if the economy's considerably improved economic performance in the second half of 1992 continues.

Both groups of fiscal activists focus mainly on government spending, while giving less attention to taxation. To the extent they address taxation issues, their emphasis is usually on distribution and "fairness," rather than supply-side incentives—that is, increasing taxation of upper-income groups and corporations, while reducing it for lower- and middle-income recipients.

In opposition to the fiscal activists are the fiscal conservatives within the Clinton administration. Their concerns focus on the overriding need to reduce the federal budget deficit from its current level of 5 percent of the gross domestic product. Among the fiscal conservatives are the secretary and deputy secretary of the treasury, Lloyd Bentsen and Roger Altman, the director and deputy directory of the Office of Management and Budget, Leon Panetta and Alice Rivlin, and the chairman of the National Economic Council, Robert Rubin.

The fiscal conservatives on the Clinton team use a collage of valid, invalid, and arguable propositions to support their view of the pernicious effects of large deficits, and the important reasons for reducing them: for example, to ease the pressure of government borrowing on bond markets and on interest rates (valid); to reduce the burdens imposed on future generations by current fiscal imbalances and the growing national debt (invalid, because these burdens largely represent payments *to* future generations of bondholders, as well as *by* future generations of taxpayers and lenders); to avoid or ease the "crowding out" of private investment and the depletion of private savings (partly valid, depending on whether deficits are reduced by cutting spending or raising taxes); and to reverse the image of an irresponsible government that is "living beyond its means" (politically valid, economically dubious). Fiscal conservatives also argue that the sort of fiscal stimulus envisaged by the nostalgic Keynesians would be inflationary and ineffective under present conditions, because structural reasons—such as low productivity growth and the trade imbalance—rather than insufficient aggregate demand account for the economy's slow growth. The fiscal conservatives will also be helped by evidence that annualized growth in the last half of 1992 exceeded 3 percent, thereby weakening the case for fiscal stimulus.

When Clinton's fiscal conservatives address tax issues their inclination is to move toward one or another form of consumption tax—such as some type of energy tax—to encourage saving. (Although partisans of Reaganomics emphasized the importance of strengthening incentives to save and invest, they and others outside the Clinton team have been reluctant to favor consumption taxation because of a fear that its power to generate huge revenues would inevitably whet Congressional appetites to boost government spending.)

Both aspects of the debate between fiscal activists and fiscal conservatives within the administration were reflected in the president's State of the Union address. The eventual outcome of this continuing debate between the insiders, as well as between them and those outside, will ultimately define Clintonomics. Predictably, the result will be a compromise: limited fiscal stimulus (for infrastructure, education, and training) that will increase government spending and will be justified as reducing the so-called "investment deficit"; partly offsetting reductions in both "discretionary" spending (defense) and "nondiscretionary" spending (entitlements, Medicare, and Medicaid); and efforts to use tax policy to slow consumption growth—for example, capping the tax deductibility of employer-provided health benefits, an energy tax, and taxing a larger proportion of Social Security income for higher income recipients. Clintonomics will be an eclectic mixture of activist and conservative ingredients. It will be less coherent than the supply-side emphasis of Reaganomics, and perhaps also less vulnerable to criticism because most potential critics will find something in the mixture that they like to offset what they don't like. On the other hand, support from potential adherents may be weakened because they find something in the mixture to dislike that offsets what they like.

April 1993

11

Social Capital and Economic Performance

One of the standard put-downs of economics and economists runs along the following lines: "About half of what economists say is right—the trouble is they don't know which half!" In the same vein, Nobel laureate Paul Samuelson, with a mixture of derision and contrition, once observed: "Economists have correctly predicted seven of the last four economic recessions."

In *Trust: The Social Virtues and the Creation of Prosperity,* Francis Fukuyama is ostensibly more generous, conceding that "neoclassical economics [is]…80 percent correct"; the "missing 20 percent of human behavior" is the concern of his provocative, insightful, and deftly written book. (I say, "ostensibly" because it seems abundantly clear from the book's content that the author means to explain considerably more than 20 percent, leaving much less than 80 percent to be credited to the economics account.)

The central thesis of *Trust* can be summarized in the following syllogism:

Premise I: High economic performance—that is, the "creation of prosperity" (and sustaining it)—is substantially helped by large, private economic organizations.

Premise II: The establishment and progress of large economic organizations (i.e., corporate giants like IBM, AT&T, Toyota, General Motors, Mitsubishi, Siemens, Daimler-Benz, etc.) is substantially helped by what Fukuyama variously refers to as "social capital," "spontaneous sociability," and "trust."

Conclusion: Therefore, high economic performance is substantially advanced by the prevalence of social capital, trust, and cultural values that sustain these qualities.

Although the syllogism conveys the essence of Fukuyama's argument, it does so at a cost of neglecting the book's broad sweep, sharp insights, and wide-ranging scholarship. As a reflection of the latter, *Trust* contains fifty-seven pages of footnotes and a twenty-page bibliography.

The breadth and scope that are missing from the syllogism are conveyed by the book's four-part structure. In Part I, Fukuyama addresses "The Idea of Trust" and the "Power of Culture" in shaping economic performance. (Part I makes plainly evident that the explanatory "power" Fukuyama ascribes to culture is considerably more than the minimal "20 percent solution" mentioned earlier.)

In Parts II and III, which comprise the 200-page core of the 362-page book, Fukuyama deals, respectively, "with "Low-Trust Societies" and "High-Trust Societies." The low-trust exemplars are China, Italy, France, and Korea, in which "familistic" Confucianism and its cognates ("Italian Confucianism"—*sic*) impede, rather that propitiate, the formation of large, private economic organizations and their attendant contributions to high economic performance. The high-trust societies are Japan and Germany, which Fukuyama ranks number one and two, according to his judgment about their respective "degrees of trust."

According to Fukuyama's argument, high-trust societies benefit from their lower transaction costs in forming the large private business organizations on which prosperity and sustained growth depend. By way of contrast, low-trust, familistic societies and cultures, such as those of China, France, Italy, and Korea, are said to confront higher transaction costs that impede the formation of such organizations. The impedance arises because the primary focus of loyalty in these societies is to the family, rather than to organizations outside of it. In seeking to overcome these obstacles and their attendant higher transaction costs, low-trust societies rely on state intervention, which turns out to be a generally poor substitute for the private organizations whose formation is inhibited.

In Part V, Fukuyama addresses the special problem posed for his thesis by American society and culture. That problem arises from the fact that, while American culture cherishes and advocates individualism, it has also "pioneered the development of the modern, hierarchical corporation," which foreshadowed the large, private business organizations whose nurturing Fukuyama extols and attributes to the pervasiveness of sociability and trust. This dilemma is resolved by Fukuyama's exposition of America's "dual" cultural heritage. Alongside America's individualistic tendencies, "which separate and atomize individuals," Fukuyama asserts, "there has been a powerful propensity to form associations and to participate in other forms of group activity."

Finally, the book concludes in Part VI with a broad-brush reconciliation between the liberal economic order envisaged as "the end of history" in Fukuyama's 1992 book of that title, and the quite different focus on cultural values and trust in his present work. As part of this reconciliation, Fukuyama advocates "the preservation and accumulation of social capital," as the essential goal of liberal civil societies.

In a book as ambitious as *Trust*, it is perhaps not surprising that its grasp falls short of its reach. A few among the numerous shortfalls are particularly worth noting.

The Absence of a Metric for Measuring Societal Trust

According to Fukuyama, societies can be characterized as "high-trust" and "low-trust, " and "social capital" can be described as something that can be "accumulated," and hence implicitly trades off against tangible capital (i.e., business investment), as well as human capital, in creating prosperity. For these concepts to be meaningful, let alone useful, there should be a *metric*: that is, a way of distinguishing between more and less, larger and smaller, increasing and decreasing. Fukuyama provides little enlightenment on this score, although several possibilities are alluded to in the course of his exposition. One of these is the number of voluntary community associations and organizations across countries and over time. But use of this as a possible proxy for measuring the amount of trust is fraught with difficulties. For example, are associations to be weighted by their membership or their duration, by their geographic scope, by their budgets, or some other measure of activity, or some combination of all of these?

Moreover, Fukuyama dismisses interest-group associations, in contrast to "voluntary associations," because the former are brought together for reasons of self-interest rather that "sociability." This seems to me a dubious distinction because many, and perhaps most, interest-group associations—like those of doctors, lawyers, economists, workers, businessmen, social scientists, engineers—involve *both* sociability and advocacy. And many so-called "voluntary associations"—like PTAs, church groups, and the Association for the United Nations—often engage in lobbying activity, as well as community sociability.

Several other candidate metrics come to mind, that are not considered in the book. One example is the size of voluntary community contributions, as well as efforts-in-kind, in response to natural disasters. (Incidentally, the Los Angeles earthquake of January 1994 elicited considerably larger community contributions than did the more devasting Kobe-Osaka earthquake of January 1995, notwithstanding the supposedly higher-trust Japanese society, compared to the presumably "lower-trust" culture of California!) Other possible metrics might include voluntary enlistments in a nation's armed forces, membership and attendance in religious groups and services, and so on. To enumerate such possible metrics only highlights their manifest shortcomings as proxy indicators of Fukuyama's concept of trust and spontaneous sociability. Yet, in a work that repeatedly makes assertions about comparative amounts and degrees of trust and sociability, the lack of explicit attention to the problem of measurement, and hence to the possible vacuity of the concept itself, is a serious flaw.

To be sure, not everything that counts can be counted, and not everything that can be counted counts. Nevertheless, in an exposition that repeatedly talks about *degrees* of trust, the *extent* of sociability, the *extent* of and *obstacles* to sociability, and the *expansion* or *erosion* of social capital, one would like to see some serious attention devoted to how to measure and reify these concepts. This is not an issue of the difference between the "touchy-feely" thinkers and the "quantoids," as one of my students has recently written. It is simply a requisite of serious analysis.

Incidentally, with such a metric or metrics to concretize the concepts that Fukuyama is elaborating, it would be entirely possible to include them in economic models to test empirically the hypotheses he advances.

Does the Central Argument Stand Up to Careful Scrutiny?

The syllogism I introduced earlier to summarize the book's central thesis can be criticized because it ignores the nuanced and allusive exposition by the author. Nevertheless, the syllogism has the advantage of exposing the essentials of the argument. When they are thus exposed, it seems clear that both the first and second premises in the syllogism, and hence the conclusion drawn from them, do not stand up to careful scrutiny.

"High economic performance" and "prosperity" can be properly defined as relatively high per capita levels of gross domestic product, or personal consumption, or sustained rates of growth, in these indicators. There is abundant empirical work indicating that these performance measures are directly dependent on high levels and rates of growth in both labor and capital productivity; and high rates of growth in labor productivity depend on increases in capital per worker and on the rate of technological progress. Productivity doesn't depend uniquely on the size of business organizations. While there are some types of efficiencies and lower transaction costs associated with large-scale organizations, there are other sorts of inefficiencies and higher transactions costs associated with large scale organizations—a point I have elaborated elsewhere.[1] Moreover, the corporate size at which scale efficiencies can be realized has been shrinking in the past decade as a result of advances in information technology, and this trend will probably continue. Recent corporate mergers and acquisitions don't contradict this point. These mergers reflect potential synergies among different business fields—for example, entertainment and telecommunications—rather than the benefits of larger size in a single field.

So, it is unpersuasive to assert, as does the first premise of the syllogism, that high performance and prosperity depend significantly on large, economic organizations.

It is also arguable whether, as the second premise of the syllogism presumes, the creation and sustenance of large economic organizations is decisively affected by "spontaneous sociability," "social capital," and the pervasiveness of "trust." There are, indeed, many other competing explanations for the prevalence, endurance, and sometimes resuscitation of large, private corporations. A participative, yet decisive, management style is one such explanation. The management styles adopted by Jack Welch at General Electric and Louis Gerstner at IBM are cases in point. Management style can do a lot to enhance the performance of large as well as small corporations, as can regular communication, clear and simple administrative rules, incentive bonuses, and even binding legal contracts—quite apart from the prevalence of "social capital" and societal "trust."

Furthermore, the syllogism's second premise is belied by common experience. For example, New York is the headquarters of some of the country's and the world's largest business corporations (IBM, Citicorp, Chevron, and others), yet it is part of New York's culture that trust and spontaneous sociability are definitely *not* part of its culture!

In the same vein, one of America's most strikingly successful companies, Walt Disney—now Disney-Capital Cities—and its charismatic CEO, Michael Eisner, flaunt a corporate culture pervaded by a minimum of trust and a maximum of internal as well as external competitiveness.

Still another counterexample is provided by a recent survey in Los Angeles that showed a rate of participation by Angelinos in community activities less than half the national average. Yet, once again, the prevalence of large business organizations in Los Angeles is manifestly higher than the average among the nation's communities.

If, then, the major and minor premises of the syllogism are spongy, then the conclusion deduced from them is compromised. Whether high economic performance depends predominantly, heavily, moderately, or slightly, if at all, on trust and "the social virtues"—whether these are 20 percent of the solution or much less—remains an open question.

Other Aspects of Culture Besides Trust

Even within the broad sociocultural domain that Fukuyama emphasizes, there are many competing perspectives, apart from trust and sociability. For example, Samuel Huntington credits "pluralism" with a major part of the explanation for Japan's successful and sustained modernization. "Pluralism," Huntington contends, "made possible the existence of people who could espouse a new way of thinking," thereby providing a "major factor in the success of Japan's modernization."

Still another sociocultural perspective is advanced by Toshiro Shimoyama, chairman of one of Japan's large corporations. He has suggested, instead, that successful modernization in Japan has been due to the absence of a religious commitment to Islam or Confucianism, rather than to sociability or trust. Others, like James Heckman and Gary Becker at Chicago have argued that a critical ingredient in high economic performance is the effectiveness of a society's educational system in building human capital.

Finally, to explain high economic performance and the creation of prosperity, such diverse commentators as Joseph Schumpeter and John Maynard Keynes, as well as recent management gurus like Tom Peters, Peter Drucker, and David Osborne, accord top billing to entrepreneurial vision and drive. And entrepreneurship—whether in large, small, or start-up firms—is no less sociocultural in character than are "trust" and "spontaneous sociability," yet is probably either independent of or even inhibited by them.

Trust concludes on a refreshingly candid note of agnosticism that can as well be applied to other sociocultural analyses of prosperity as to Fukuyama's own. "What we can say," Fukuyama concludes, "is that the impact of cultural differences in the propensity for sociability will have a large, but at the moment indeterminate, impact on economic life."

Fall 1995

Note

1. See "The New Mercantilism," *The Public Interest,* Summer 1994 (chapter 3 above).

12

"Downsizing," Corporate Responsibility, and the Trade-Off Between Efficiency and Equity

Downsizings in corporate America typically result after newly appointed CEOs, or tardily alerted incumbents, confront and resolve a harsh dilemma: either heed the message transmitted by their corporate profit-and-loss accounts, or be replaced by someone who will. Resolution of the dilemma usually results in a situation that can be summarized by a parable.

Suppose a firm's profit-and-loss accounts show that its revenues from sales have not changed or have increased only slightly between this year and the previous one, while its net earnings have risen enormously—say, doubled. Assume further that circumstances external to the firm's own operations haven't changed materially—for example, the firm's sales volume hasn't changed, prices haven't increased, and the firm's product line is unchanged. So, it follows that the firm's costs must have been significantly reduced, thereby explaining the big jump in earnings notwithstanding constant revenues.

This explanation can be described in various ways that differ in clarity and tact, but are essentially similar in content and meaning. For example, one can say simply that the firm has become more efficient. Or that waste has been reduced or eliminated. Or that resources, including people, have been "downsized," or that the production process has been "reengineered." Whatever the vocabulary that is used to make the point, it is unequivocally clear that downsizing generally raises the productivity of the labor and other resources that remain employed by the firm. And increased productivity is, fundamentally, what a rising standard of living and the economy's growth depend on.

Predictably these buoyant effects on the firm's P&L accounts will be accompanied or followed by an increase in the market value of the firm's stock and its shareholders' assets, as well as a probable boost in its dividends. Also in train are likely to be large (sometimes huge) jumps in compensation of top executives, because these are usually linked through options and bonuses to the firm's market value and its net earnings, respectively.

This oft-repeated downsizing scenario has recurred innumerable times throughout the American economy, in the process strengthening the international competitive position of American firms and increasing the U.S. role as the world's largest exporting economy.

Yet, these developments also create acute problems that reverberate in the country's quotidian politics and rhetoric. The problems concern the diminution of job security, and the proper role of corporate responsibility in the downsizing scenario. While the value of shareholders' "equities" goes up, dismissed workers and the communities in which they live find that their "equity" has gone down. The result is a widely shared view that the entire process is unfair because it is one in which shareholders (and management) benefit at the expense of "stakeholders" (workers and communities), while corporate responsibility to the latter is abjured. This view is reinforced by the highly publicized dismissals or induced retirements of thousands of workers and mid-level managers at AT&T, IBM, Nynex-Bell Atlantic, Chase-Chemical, Wells Fargo-Interstate, Lockheed-Martin, and other corporations that have streamlined or merged their operations in recent months.

To be sure, less than 2 percent of the entire U.S. labor force has been directly affected each year, aggregate employment has continued to rise, and the national unemployment rate has remained low—most recently hovering around the so-called "natural" (i.e., minimum "nonaccelerating-inflation-rate-of-unemployment") rate of 5.5 percent. Moreover, the average duration of unemployment, between dismissals and reemployment, remains very low—about four to five months in the U.S., compared with more than sixteen months in the European economies where total unemployment is about twice the U.S. figure. Nevertheless, these *average* figures belie the fact that the impact and hardships accompanying downsizing have been concentrated in particular regions and among particular segments of the population. And the perception of unfairness has been accentuated by the angst-ridden rhetoric expressed at both ends of the political spectrum: from Pat Buchanan to Jesse Jackson, from Pat Robertson to Robert Reich.

Moreover, the perception of unfairness—that the "haves" are getting more, while the "have-nots" are getting less—is reinforced by empirical evidence, quite separate from downsizing itself, that the distribution of income and wealth has generally become more unequal. Whereas the upper fifth of the income distribution received 41.5 percent of aggregate family income in 1980, it received 46.2 percent in 1993. In contrast, the lower fifth of the distribution received 5.2 percent of aggregate family income in 1980 compared with only 4.2 percent in 1993.

What part of the real and perceived consequences of generic "downsizing" should be placed at the door marked "corporate responsibility," and what part should be lodged with the individual or with society-at-large?

Despite the prevalence of strongly held and often stridently expressed beliefs, no formulary answer is convincing. What can be said is that corporate responsibility to "stakeholders" should embrace at least those aspects of downsizings that affect reasonable business calculations: for example, by affecting the morale and productivity of retained workers through provision of ample advance warning to those to be laid off, by affording reasonable retraining opportunities that may reduce the number of layoffs, and by efforts to obtain a sufficient level of understanding and acceptance in the community to avoid impairment of the downsizing firms' market position. In the absence of this minimal level of concern by corporate management, consumers may be activated to take retaliatory actions that would be detrimental to the interests of *both* shareholders and stakeholders.

July 1996

Part II

Economic Power and Military Power

13

Competing Priorities in the Post-Cold War Era

Despite fractious disagreement on nearly all current issues—from Bosnia to China, and from welfare to Medicare—one view is widely shared by liberals and conservatives, Democrats and Republicans, academics and journalists, labor and management, internationalists and neo-isolationists: in the post-cold war world, economics matters more and military affairs less than before.

Despite the consensus, this view is profoundly misleading, if not demonstrably wrong.

To be sure, the world has changed drastically. The overarching threat posed by the Soviet Union's huge, alert nuclear forces is gone, as is the conventional threat posed by the Warsaw Pact's preponderant conventional forces facing those of NATO. These dramatic changes significantly reduce, if not erase, the corresponding military threats and challenges. Yet this does not warrant the usual inference that military issues have diminished in importance relative to economic ones, nor that public policy should be more concerned with the latter than the former.

This inference is unwarranted for two principal reasons. First, the range and gravity of the military issues and problems that cohabit the post-cold war world are more numerous and more serious than is usually recognized. Second, while the contemporaneous economic issues and problems are also substantial, many of them can and will be ameliorated by market forces: there is no self-correcting mechanism operating to mitigate military challenges and problems that corresponds to the operation of market forces in mitigating economic challenges and problems.

Even an abbreviated inventory of the salient military issues, risks, and potential conflicts that characterize the post-cold war era, suggests how numerous and formidable they are. This inventory includes the following elements:

- Possession by twenty-four nations (besides the United States, France, and the United Kingdom) of ballistic missile delivery capabilities, with range extensions in varying stages of development that could reach the United States and its closest allies.

- Proliferation of advanced conventional weapons, including sea- and air-delivered missiles, submarines, and air-defense systems, through foreign weapons sales by major suppliers (including those in the United States), as well as sales of dual-use technologies that expand the number of potential producers of these weapons.

- Proliferation of weapons of mass destruction—nuclear, biological, and chemical—potentially coupled with the longer-range missile delivery technology referred to above.

- China's assertion of sovereignty in the Spratly Islands and throughout the South China Sea, combined with expansion and modernization of its military capabilities, especially naval capabilities. (China's recent missile-testing exercises in the Taiwan Straits provided an unsubtle testimonial to these developments.)

- The perennial conflicts in the Balkans, which may abate or may just as likely spread beyond their recent battlegrounds.

- North Korea's still-threatening conventional military posture vis-à-vis South Korea, as well as the major uncertainties connected with its agreement to halt and roll back development of its nuclear weapons capabilities.

- Russia's reduced, yet still large, military capabilities, and its continued development of new and improved naval and air weapons.

One thing that's clear about this abbreviated list of major military issues and challenges is that there is no benign mechanism that operates to mitigate them, as there is—however imperfectly it operates—in the case of economic issues and challenges. Economic issues, and the disputes they often entail between, say, the U.S. and Japan, or the U.S. and the European Union, can frequently be eased or circumvented by the self-interested actions of business firms, entrepreneurial zeal, and international corporate alliances, operating in response to market incentives.

When the Sumitomo Bank asks the Ford Motor Company to help reorganize Mazda, and thereby protect their joint holdings in the Japanese company, the Ford-Sumitomo partnership is contributing to easing the sometimes antagonistic economic confrontation between their respective governments, while also advancing the partners' interests.

When Toyota and Nissan agree to purchase more auto parts from the United States and to shift some production of passenger vehicles to the U.S., they are impelled as much by the overvalued yen as the overcharged negotiating rhetoric employed by the U.S. and Japanese governments.

When IBM, Toshiba, and Siemens collaborate in designing, producing, and marketing the next generation 64-megabit memory chip and its prospective 256-megabit successor, they are directly advancing their separate and joint interests, while indirectly forging welcome linkages between the U.S., Japanese, and European economies.

And as the Disney-Capital Cities/ABC merger finds new ways to expand in the Japanese entertainment and recreational market beyond the successful record of Disney's Orayasu theme park outside Tokyo, these mutually profitable endeavors will provide an emollient for the inevitable trade frictions that will occur between the U.S. and Japanese governments.

The large and growing network of such international, interfirm alliances doesn't signal the "end of the nation state," as Kenichi Ohmae's recent book of that title suggests. But it does sharply differentiate economic issues and disputes, which can often be transcended by a combination of entrepreneurial ingenuity and self-correcting market incentives, from military issues and disputes which cannot be. Negotiations (sometimes acrimonious) and agreements (sometimes ambiguous) among the respective governments are not always necessary, and sometimes not even fruitful, to alleviate economic frictions among these parties.

Conventional wisdom is sometimes, as in this instance, misleading: despite the prevailing consensus to the contrary, there is no convincing basis for asserting that public policy and public discussion should accord military issues and challenges lesser importance or lower priority than that accorded economic issues and challenges.

August 1995

14

Military Power, Economic Power, and a Less Disorderly World

Prior to Desert Storm and Desert Shield, it had become fashionable in some intellectual and political circles, as well as in the media, to predict the receding importance of military power, and its replacement by economic power in the hierarchy of global policy instruments.

Developments in the Middle East since August 1990 have silenced, perhaps only temporarily, the earlier rhetoric about the obsolescence of military power. Nevertheless, while these developments have strikingly demonstrated the importance of military power, the Gulf War also demonstrated an equally important point about the crucial role of economic power.

Economic instruments of power—including capital, technology, goods and services—are intimately linked with those of military power. And the linkages are often complex, subtle, and significant. Economic power often complements military power, rather than substituting for it, although there are also instances where each can substitute for the other. The converse proposition—that military power often complements economic power—is no less true. (As physicist Niels Bohr once observed, the opposite of a shallow truth is false, while the opposite of a deep truth can also be true.)

In the specific case of the Gulf War, economic power was a vital adjunct of military power. Curtailment of Iraq's access to oil revenues and to imports contributed to weakening its capabilities for resistance. And economic interests and incentives provided important elements in bonding the extraordinary U.S.-led, twenty-nine-nation coalition engaged in Desert Shield and Desert Storm. Forgiveness of Egypt's $7 billion military debt to the United States, as well as the promise of more direct economic support in the future, were important in enlisting and sustain-

73

ing Egypt's vital role in the coalition. Assurance to Turkey that it would receive offsets to the economic sacrifices it made in embargoing oil deliveries from Iraq played a similarly crucial role in facilitating its participation in the coalition.

Although the Soviet Union's direct participation in the coalition was limited—confined to a couple of naval vessels in the Gulf to help enforce the embargo against Iraq—its political role in supporting the twelve Security Council resolutions was important. To be sure, this role became somewhat tendentious, if not mischievous, in the final stages of the war. Nevertheless, the generally supportive stance of the Union government was valuable, and doubtless was influenced by Soviet interest in avoiding anything that might further impair its access to Western trade, technology, and finance.

In a similar vein, other members of the diverse coalition—notably, Syria, Pakistan, Czechoslovakia, and Poland—were surely influenced by considerations of economic interest and access. In these cases, economic leverage contributed to enhancing military effectiveness. In other instances, the causality runs the other way. A case in point has been Saudi Arabia's steadfast resistance in the war's aftermath to OPEC pressure to reduce oil production and raise oil prices. Thus, the U.S. military effort to protect Saudi security has resulted in economic benefits to the United States, as well as other oil importers.

The closeness, as well as complexity, of the linkages between economic and military power are also exemplified by the anomalous roles of Japan and Germany in the Gulf crisis. Both countries opted to provide funds rather than forces, due to real or alleged political constraints that hindered their deployment of forces abroad. To this extent, economic instruments substituted, although imperfectly, for military ones. However, from the standpoint of the coalition as a whole, the Japanese and German financial commitments—which still remain to be fully implemented—helped to support the coalition by providing economic benefits (or relief from costs) for several of the "frontline" states whose military participation would otherwise have been more problematic.

In the war's murky aftermath, the interplay between economic and military instruments is also crucial. Constructing, protecting, and supplying enclaves for the Kurds has depended on the coordinated use of economic and military measures. If a durable political solution is to be found to the plight of the majority Kurdish and Shi'ite populations of

Iraq, the solution will require a combined application of military and economic instruments by countries within and outside the Middle East.

For the United States and other countries to make progress in fashioning a less disorderly world, if not a "new world order," coalitions and collective institutions that prominently involve Third World countries, as well as others, will be of central importance. And economic as well as military instruments will be essential in bringing such coalitions and institutions into being, or in revitalizing existing ones, whether within or outside the United Nations. If this process is to be effective, the economic and military instruments of power will have to be carefully coordinated. They will often turn out to be closely complementary, rather than in opposition, to one another.

May 1991

15

Economics and Security in Central Europe

One proposition distinguishing the post-cold war era from the past is that economics matters relatively more, and military power less, than before. Moreover, economic issues have now become more closely and directly linked to security concerns. While these general propositions are widely accepted, specific examples and applications are rarely offered. We propose a specific and important instance of this linkage.

The stability and security of the four Central and Eastern European countries—Poland, Hungary, and the Czech and Slovakian republics (the so-called Visegrad-Four)—depend no less on their economic condition and prospects (and, in turn, on their access to Western markets), than on assurances against military threats.

Yet a disproportionate amount of policy debate and press attention has, in the wake of President Clinton's recent European trip, been devoted to the military dimension compared to that devoted to the economic dimension. This balance needs to be redressed.

Prospects for security and stability, as well as for prosperity and democracy, in the V-4 countries will be significantly enhanced by a double-track strategy that, on the economic track, increasingly links them with the EC (or European Union as the EC is now officially known) as well as GATT and, on the security track, links them with NATO (through the North Atlantic Cooperation Council [NACC] and through President Clinton's "Partnership for Peace"). Moreover, progress on each track will be abetted by pursuing them in parallel and in balance with one other. Unfortunately, and inappropriately, the two tracks are too often discussed and pursued separately.

Coauthored with Harold Brown.

Increased and sustained economic growth in the V-4 will contribute to their internal stability and security, and these goals will be helped more by expanded trade—specifically by expanded access of their exports to the markets of the European Community—than by foreign aid. Global exports by the V-4 countries are about $35 billion, of which about half already goes to the EC. Although this share has increased in the past two years, V-4 exports to the EC are constrained by the Community's agricultural tariffs and industrial quotas limiting V-4 exports of agricultural and meat products, textiles, and steel. These restrictions are supposed to be eased during the remainder of the decade. Were they to be rapidly removed, rather than gradually eased, the potential for expanding V-4 exports to EC markets would be substantial—perhaps 30 to 40 percent in the near term future. Although U.S. extension of MFN status to the V-4 countries will also result in some increase in their trade with the U.S., the potential for expansion in EC markets is much greater. Such a rapid expansion of exports by the V-4 countries over the next two or three years could boost their real growth by 3 or 4 percentage points—increasing their annual GDP growth rates by about one-third. Moreover, as the growth of V-4 trade accelerates, it can be expected that foreign direct investments in the four countries—estimated at about $2.4 billion in 1993—also will be stimulated.

The combined effects of such increased economic growth and foreign investment in the V-4 countries would significantly enhance political and social stability and internal security.

The EC decided in June 1993 that the V-4 could become full members of the Community at an unspecified future time, when they have "met the conditions for membership." Although an argument could be made that one or more of the V-4 already meet the "conditions for membership" to a greater extent than at least one of the present EC members, the argument is beside the point. The EC can and will decide whether and when to admit additional members. Nevertheless, the EC could, in the interim, grant the V-4 countries the greater market access that we propose, without admitting them as full EC members

Increased market access by the V-4 countries is in the long-term national and collective interests of the EC as well as of the United States because of the impetus this will provide to progress, stability and security in Central and Eastern Europe, and to full integration of the V-4 countries in the world economy.

Expanded V-4 market access should be deliberately synchronized with an expansion of their military linkages with NATO—through joint planning, joint military exercises, enlarged military training programs, and perhaps some joint military R&D efforts—under the aegis of NACC and PFP. Synchronization of the economic and military efforts will enhance their mutual effectiveness because progress and confidence gained in one sphere will contribute to progress and confidence in the other.

Security issues arise from both the end of the Warsaw Pact and the disjunction between ethnic and state boundaries in Central and Eastern Europe. The terrible but instructive examples of former Yugoslavia and the Caucasus may have discouraged overt conflict, but the possibility remains. Fears of a possible resurgent Russian expansionism led the Visegrad countries (and others further east) to request NATO membership, with its Article 5 commitment ("an attack on one is an attack on all"). But the Russians surely know that any such attempt on their part would revive the cold war. Although eventual NATO membership of the Visegrad countries should not be ruled out, the NATO leaders at their meeting on January 10th and 11th, plainly wished to avoid the anti-Russian message that such an action might convey, lest it strengthen the anti-democratic and irredentist forces in Russia and thus become a self-fulfilling apprehension. The NATO Cooperation Council, which includes NATO nations plus all former Warsaw Pact members and all the states of the former Soviet Union, provides a forum for dialogue, although it is too heterogeneous to be more than a forum for dialogue.

The "Partnership for Peace" proposal goes an appropriate step further by allowing military cooperation, extending to joint exercises, and more fuzzily to peacekeeping. It asserts a NATO interest in Central European security. A commitment for consultation on possible action against aggression would be a reasonable future step. Each such decision on a country-by-country basis would involve an uncomfortable drawing of lines, with Russia and most or all other states of the FSU on the other side. Hence, Russian sensitivities require that we seek Russian acknowledgment and consultation, coupled perhaps with a Russia-specific "partnership for peace" with NATO out-of-area, for example in the Balkans or the Persian Gulf. These uncertainties and ambiguities reinforce the notion that pursuit of this lengthy process is even more important than the exact nature of its early stages.

For Central Europe, the security and economic paths should be pursued in parallel because they complement one another. Investments by the West, especially direct investments by Western European and American firms so necessary to the economic development, stability and strengthened democracy of Central Europe, will flow only if there is confidence in its security. That security in turn depends on internal stability, democratization, and economic progress as well as on assurances against external domination. Now that "Partnership for Peace" has been adopted, action to provide access to Western European and North American markets would be the most valuable contribution to V-4 security, because of the economic progress and internal stability it would promote.

January 1994

16

Economic Instruments, Military Instruments, and National Power

Among the extraordinary changes that have occurred in the international arena since the late 1980s, three sets of events have provided particular support for several now widely accepted propositions pertaining to economic and military policies, national interests, and national power. The three events are the advent of *perestroika* in 1986 and its consequences, including the dissolution of the Soviet Union; the fall of the Wall in 1989 and its consequences in Central and Eastern Europe; and Japan's dramatic economic performance, as well as the associated occurrence of large and sustained current account deficits by the United States and surpluses by Japan.

The widely accepted propositions are:

1. Economic interests, issues, and instruments are becoming increasingly important and influential in international affairs.
2. Military issues, interests, and instruments are becoming less important and influential.
3. U.S. national power—at least, the salient (economic) dimension of that power—has declined and/or is declining relative to that of other countries.
4. This decline is due to overemphasis on military issues and instruments.
5. "Reversal," "renewal," and "revitalizing" of U.S. power and influence depend on redressing this misplaced emphasis by focusing more on economic issues and economic policy instruments.

Among the best illustrations of these views are the following:
From Samuel Huntington:

> In this new environment...military capabilities are likely to be less important than they have been in the past. Economic measures will be central...diplomacy

81

and economics will be crucial...the promotion of U.S. strategic interests will involve not only foreign and defense policy but also domestic policy on the budget, taxes, subsidies, industrial policy, science and technology, child care, education, and other topics.

The one area of U.S. weakness is economics and the challenge in that arena comes from Japan. In a world where economic power and economic issues are increasingly important, that challenge is a real one.[1]

From Paul Kennedy:

[B]ecause a top-heavy military establishment may slow down the rate of economic growth and lead to a decline in the nation's share of world manufacturing output, and therefore wealth, and therefore *power*, the whole issue becomes of the [sic] balancing the short-term security afforded by large defense forces against the longer-term security of rising production and income.[2]

[T]he United States now runs the risk, so familiar to historians of the rise and fall of previous Great Powers, of what might roughly be called "imperial overstretch": that is to say, decision-makers in Washington must face the awkward and enduring fact that the sum total of the United States' global interests and obligations is nowadays far larger than the country's power to defend them all simultaneously.[3]

From John Mueller:

Throughout the developed world countries are coming to the conclusion that the most desirable thing to have, after such basic concerns as life and security are taken care of, is prosperity. That is, just about everybody would rather be rich than just about anything else.[4]

From my RAND colleague, David Ochmanek:

As the Soviet threat atrophies, there will be less willingness on both sides of the Pacific to compromise on what used to be seen as second-tier issues. We who work on national security issues have long consigned trade and burdensharing to the second tier, focusing on deterrence of the Soviet Union and arms control in the first tier. Now these are becoming secondary or tertiary, and trade, burdensharing, and cooperation on the environment are the first-tier issues.[5]

I agree with many of these propositions and citations. They contain much truth, but what they contain is not the whole truth.

There are three reasons why at least some reservations about their validity is warranted. First, the precise meaning of some of the terms is not clear and hence some of the propositions are ambiguous. Second, the propositions seem too simple to deal adequately with the complex phenomena they purport to describe and explain. Third, errors and miscues have so often in recent years followed in the wake of commonly accepted assertions and forecasts that it is probably worthwhile to be skeptical about the validity of this new area of apparent consensus.

In this chapter, I will begin to address these matters in several ways: trying to clarify some of the ambiguous terminology, suggesting various ways of measuring—or at least thinking about measuring—the terms that are used, and proposing several simple and explicit hypotheses about the relationships and interactions among the terms and concepts.

Central Theme, Terminology, Measurement

My central thesis is that economic and military instruments of power are intimately linked, rather than each being independent of the other, or one being clearly and invariably dominant over the other; that the relationships between them are often complex and subtle; and that these relationships vary in different post-cold war contexts. Economic power, to be effective, sometimes complements (reinforces, or even requires) military power or may be complemented by military power, and at other times and in other circumstances, can substitute for it. The converse proposition is also valid: sometimes military power can substitute for economic power, and at other times and in other circumstances, military power may complement (reinforce, or require) economic power. (Niels Bohr once observed that the opposite of a shallow truth is false, while the opposite of a deep truth can also be true.) Because of these interactive relationships, it may be unwise to consign military power to abrupt neglect or precipitous decline.

I will first define these terms, and then explore the hypothesized relationships among them.

Several plausible indicators or metrics can be used, at a very aggregative level, to define and size what I mean by "economic instruments" of power: GNP, population (and hence labor supply and per capita GNP), and a country's current account surplus. GNP and per capita GNP are typically used by the previously cited authors in their references to economic power, or to changes among countries in their relative economic power. I have added the current account surplus as an economic instrument of power on the arguable premise that it represents a capital resource that, in principle at least, can be guided or shunted, by the use of one policy device or another, toward or away from a particular target area that may be the object of a nation's power.

At a more disaggregative level, the economic instruments of power can be defined in terms of components of the GNP that are believed to be particularly significant—for example, advanced and advancing technology sectors such as telecommunications, microelectronics, semiconductors, fiber optics, engineering and bioengineering industries—whose special significance resides in the economy-wide, growth-promoting effects they are thought to generate, in the monopoly market power (and supernormal profits) they may entail, or in their putative connection to present or future military capabilities. Similarly, specific components of the population and manpower pool may be considered of greater significance as economic instruments of power than the population as a whole: for example, certain types of skilled labor; managers; design, production, and marketing engineers; and of course economists and policy analysts. One can also think of more disaggregative components of a country's international accounts as providing another type of economic power: for example, the size of its market to which foreign access may be permitted or denied. This can be roughly proxied by its level of imports. (Note that a country's level of *imports* are—potentially, at least—a source of economic power, not just its exports.) Another component is the volume of exports of goods and services that a country can direct toward or exclude from foreign areas.

Economic instruments of national power provide a means of influencing behavior by conferring rewards or imposing penalties. For example, a country's capacity to provide economic assistance or to apply economic sanctions by withholding or denying trade or assistance depends on what I have defined as its economic instruments.

Indicators of a country's "military instruments" of power are, at an aggregative level, its military spending, the size and quality of its military forces (active and reserve), and the magnitude of its military capital stock. At a more disaggregative level, the military instruments entail specific types of forces and capabilities: for example, air and sea lift; projection forces; accurate delivery systems; command, control, and intelligence capabilities; and so on.

Military instruments of national power provide a means of influencing behavior in the international arena by deterrence or compellence; that is, by using force, or a credible threat to use it, to dissuade other countries from using force; or by using force to coerce, preempt, or repel their attempts to use it.

Before being criticized for neglecting the important role of political and diplomatic instruments of power, I will simply acknowledge that I take their importance for granted. I do not mean to imply that the political and diplomatic instruments are less important than the ones I have referred to, nor that they also interact with the economic and military instruments in complex and substitutive, as well as potentially reinforcing, ways. But I want to focus here more directly on the economic and military instruments of power because much of the recent discussion about the new and changing international "order," and much of the previously cited literature, have this focus. In the following discussion, I will abstract from the acknowledged effects of political and diplomatic instruments to concentrate on the economic and military ones.[6] This should not be construed as discounting or diminishing the importance of politics and diplomacy, but as a departure from realism in the interests of convenience.

To continue this glossary, I define "power" as a generalized and more or less "convertible" asset capable, within limits, of protecting and advancing national interests. I will not have much to say about "national interests." To the extent that references to them occur in what I have already said, I construe national interests as very broad goals and principles—for example, "life, liberty, and the pursuit of happiness" or, alternatively, military security, freedom, and prosperity. Defining national interests in more operationally useful terms depends on particular policy contexts and circumstances that I will not be addressing here, although I will make some brief observations later about the relation between national or public interests, and private ones.

In defining power as an asset that can be used to protect and advance national interests, I am avoiding the question of willingness or motivation to use it.[7] Thus, while the magnitude or "value" of U.S. power may be large (and may actually have grown in relative terms), our willingness to use it may have receded as a result of the end of the cold war and the dissolution of the Soviet Union, as well as our increasing disposition to attend to serious problems at home rather than those abroad.

I have not been able to think of a suitable metric for national "power" that is independent of the contributory instruments. If one thinks of power as a convertible asset capable of protecting and advancing national interests by influencing behavior, specific examples of the exercise of that power can be cited, as well as instances in which there were serious limitations on its exercise and effectiveness. For example, the United States demonstrated its power in organizing the Desert Shield/Desert Storm coalition, and applying that power to bring about a stipulated goal: ejection of Iraq from Kuwait. U.S. power—economic as well as military—has also been largely—if arguably—responsible for victory in the cold war and the disestablishment of communism in the former Soviet Union. Recent efforts to bring about peace and stability in the Middle East by bringing Arabs and Israelis to the negotiating table have exemplified the extent of U.S. power as well as its limitations. Other illustrations of the limitations on U.S. power abound: for example, U.S. removal from naval and air bases in the Philippines; the inordinate delays and difficulty encountered in trying to bring about a phased removal of export subsidies in agricultural trade and eventual completion of the Uruguay Round of GATT; inability to bring about successful outcomes in Bosnia, Somalia, Haiti, etc.; our limited ability to control international sales of conventional weapons or to stop proliferation of nuclear, chemical, and biological weapons technology, and so on.

Before too much is made of these limitations on U.S. power, it is worth recalling that even during much of the 1960s and 1970s when the United States was supposedly "hegemonic," our ability to influence external events along lines we desired was no less, and perhaps even more, limited. Recall, for example, that a Marxist-Leninist regime became firmly entrenched in Cuba at the start of the 1960s; that nuclear weapons were acquired by France (1960), China (1964), and India (1974), despite strong U.S. opposition; that France exited from NATO in 1967; and that South Vietnam was overrun by Communist North Vietnam in 1975. If one compares the period of our supposed hegemonic past with the period of supposed U.S. decline in the 1980s and early 1990s (in which the cold war has been won, the Soviet military threat has eroded, communism has been crumbling, and democratization and marketization are advancing, if sometimes falteringly), it can be argued that our effective "power" has been greater in the recent period of supposed decline than in the prior one of putative hegemony!

Relationships and Interactions

Having more or less clearly defined the terms, I hypothesize three sets of relationships among them:

- First, in a given context, the national "power" of the United States depends on (is a function of) its economic instruments, military instruments, and a set of other "shift" variables, including in particular the political and diplomatic ones.[8]
- Second, economic instruments depend on the level of economic instruments existing in the preceding period, the level of military instruments in the current period, and a set of other influencing factors or variables, such as the GNP, its division between investment and consumption, its growth rate, or particularly significant sectors or components of the GNP.[9]
- The third relationship stipulates that the level of military instruments depends on the level of military instruments in the preceding period, the current level of economic instruments, and a set of other influencing factors or variables, such as alliance relationships, political and social cohesion, and so on.[10]

The second and third relationships reflect comments I made earlier: the effectiveness of economic instruments depends in part on the military instruments, and vice versa.

I will not conjecture about the possible functional forms of these relationships, whether they are additive or multiplicative, whether and when they are subject to increasing or decreasing returns, and so on. In general, the national power specified in the first relationship will be greater when the economic instruments or the military instruments are larger. In some circumstances, one of these may substitute for the other. In other circumstances, more of one instrument will have little or no effect on "power" without an increment of the other (complementarity). Examples of both situations are offered later.

The relationship that defines the economic instruments (equation [2]) is also complex. To the extent that the military instruments take resources away from the economic instruments, the relation between them is negative and conflicting. To the extent that military instruments (for example, military technology or foreign military sales) may generate spillovers that benefit the economy at large or particular sectors within it, the relationship between them is positive and synergistic. A similar complexity applies to the functional relationship between the military instruments and the economic instruments in the third hypothesis. Resources devoted to economic instruments reduce those available for military instruments, but the economic instruments may also raise the effectiveness of resources (e.g., technology) devoted to the military instruments.[11]

Examples and Illustrations

The complex and varying relationships between economic and military instruments of national power can be illustrated by examples from the recent past, as well as by their application to potential and current national security issues.

One aspect of these relationships is illustrated by a security problem that will be increasingly serious in the new and not necessarily orderly world environment: namely, the problem of establishing and enforcing controls on arms shipments to various regions, especially arms trade involving weapons of mass destruction. To begin with, one can use standard force-on-force analysis to establish one or more stable military balances at different levels of regional military forces. This problem is not unfamiliar, although it has certain complicating characteristics in some regions. For example, in the Middle East, stability must be sufficiently robust to meet the test of different and possibly changing combinations of potential adversaries, rather than a single and static adversarial alignment. However, let us assume that such more or less stable force balances can be calculated, and that they would be reassuring rather than threatening to all members of the region.

The question then arises, how might these balances be enforced by controlling weapons *imports* into the countries of the region, and similarly, by controlling *exports* from the weapons suppliers? If arms import "quotas" for different categories of weapons can be established for each country of the region (derived from the prior analysis of stable balances), then perhaps it may be possible to enforce those quotas by using, for example, the extension or threatened withholding of economic assistance as inducements for compliance by the importing countries, or by using technical assistance to provide improved defense budgeting processes for the countries of the region, to increase transparency and accountability, to facilitate collective monitoring of military transactions, and thereby contribute to compliance. In this case, a military instrument—arms control as a contributor to stable deterrence—might be strengthened (complemented) by the use of economic instruments.

Inducing compliance by the sellers—both the G-5 principal ones and the second-tier ones (e.g., Brazil, Argentina, Korea, Taiwan)—is at least as difficult as inducing compliance by the buyers. Consistent with establishing quotas for the types and quantities of arms imports by regional buyers, export quotas might be agreed upon by the arms sellers, analogous to producer agreements that have been negotiated and maintained for many years (with varying success) in connection with internationally traded commodities such as tin and coffee. Enforcement of regional arms export quotas might be accomplished by invoking another economic instrument: namely, the threat of excluding firms that engage in quota-breaking sales from access to the U.S. market. This would be another instance of using economic instruments to complement military ones.

Economic instruments will also affect the direct employment of force in the post-cold war era. Effective use of force is likely to be increasingly dependent upon collaborative participation among several countries acting in concert. Whether this collaboration occurs through the United Nations or through *ad hoc* coalitions—Desert Shield/Storm reflected both elements—the ability to form such coalitions will increasingly be influenced by the use of economic instruments to provide rewards or to impose or threaten economic penalties.

In the specific case of Desert Shield and Desert Storm, economic instruments of power were vital adjuncts of the military instruments that were employed. For example, curtailment of Iraq's access to oil revenues and to imports of equipment and spare parts probably contributed to weakening its capabilities for resistance. And economic instruments and incentives provided important elements in bonding the extraordinary U.S.-led, twenty-nine-nation coalition engaged in Desert Shield and Desert Storm. Forgiving Egypt's $7 billion military debt to the United States, as well as extending a promise of more direct economic support in the future, was an important inducement to enlist and sustain Egypt's crucial role in the coalition. Assurance to Turkey that it would receive offsets to the economic sacrifices it made in embargoing oil deliveries from Iraq played a similarly crucial role in facilitating its participation in the coalition.

Although the Soviet Union's direct participation in the Gulf coalition was limited—confined to a couple of naval vessels in the Gulf to help enforce the embargo against Iraq—its political role was crucial in supporting the twelve Security Council resolutions. To be sure, this role became somewhat tendentious, if not mischievous, in the final stages of the war. Nevertheless, the generally supportive stance of the then-Union government was valuable, and doubtless was influenced by Soviet interest in avoiding anything that might further impair its access to Western trade, technology, and finance.

In a similar vein, other members of the diverse coalition—notably Syria, Pakistan, Czechoslovakia, and Poland—were probably influenced by considerations of economic interest and access. In these cases, economic instruments contributed to enhancing the effectiveness of military ones. In other instances, the causality has run the other way. For example, Saudi Arabia's steadfast resistance, after the Gulf war, to OPEC pressure to reduce oil production and raise oil prices, suggests the reverse causal sequence. In this case, the U.S. military effort to protect Saudi security against the threat from Iraq resulted in economic benefits—an enhancement of U.S. economic instruments—as well as benefits to other oil importers.

The closeness, as well as complexity, of the linkages between economic and military instruments was also exemplified by the anomalous roles of Japan and Germany. Both countries opted to provide funds rather than forces due to real or alleged political constraints that hindered their deployment of forces abroad. To this extent, their economic instruments substituted, albeit imperfectly, for military ones. From the standpoint of the coalition as a whole, the significant Japanese and German financial commitments helped to support the coalition by providing economic benefits (or relief from costs) for several of the "front line" states whose military participation would otherwise have been more uncertain.

Concluding Observations

Some of the relationships between economic and military instruments can be summarized in several propositions—some of which are deducible from the preceding discussion, while others are not. Some of the propositions support and supplement those stated at the beginning of this chapter, while others do not.

1. The international environment of the post-cold war era will be characterized by uncertainty, unpredictability, and instability. Many, and probably most, of the instabilities will warrant a response from the United States of neglect—benign or otherwise—either on grounds of limitations on our power to bring about predictable improvement and relief, or on grounds of limited national interests in trying to do so. But some instabilities may warrant the application of either or both economic and military instruments, by the United States acting alone or, more likely, acting in coalition with others. *To choose when and how to respond in such*

circumstances will entail a capacity for resilience and flexibility in the design and deployment of economic and military instruments—both separately and in combination.

2. In an environment in which uncertainty (in the sense of incalculability rather than of probabilistic "risk") will be greater, and a higher premium will be placed on "resilience" and flexibility, *the economic instruments of power may be of increased importance relative to the military instruments.* (To be more precise, the respective partial derivatives of power with respect to the economic instruments will probably rise relative to those with respect to the military instruments in the functional relationships described above.) The ability to confer economic advantages or impose economic penalties will be preferred over the ability to coerce, although the latter will sometimes augment the effectiveness of the former.

3. The contention that U.S. domestic socioeconomic problems (which affect the magnitudes of the economic instruments, as defined above), are due principally to overemphasis on the military instruments is not tenable. Resources devoted to military instruments in the United States over the last several decades have varied from 3 or 4 percent to 6 or 7 percent. The resources that would be freed by lower levels of military spending would inevitably be divided between consumption and investment, with the former probably absorbing most of the savings (or peace "dividend"). Hence, the predictable incremental effect on GNP growth would be less than half of one percent per annum. Rather than resulting from the magnitude and composition of the military instruments, the socioeconomic problems that impede economic growth and "competitiveness" depend instead on many other complex and troublesome problems and issues that are quite unrelated to the military variables: for example, tax policies, education policies and institutions, health care financing, and "governance" (for example, term limits, campaign funding, executive-congressional relations, and federal-state-local government relations).

4. As already noted, economic performance is minimally affected by whether as little as 3 percent of the GNP or as much as 6 percent of it is allocated for military instruments. To the extent that sustained economic performance is equated with what is sometimes referred to as economic "security," its determinants are largely matters of domestic policy rather than foreign policy.

5. The earlier statement that national "power" can be thought of as a "convertible" asset that can be used to protect and advance national in-

terests has begged the question of defining "national interests" in a meaningful way. While it is legitimate and valid to link national interests to the broad national purposes and values mentioned above, at this high level of generality "national interests" have limited influence on policy because they can usually be invoked to justify widely different policy positions.[12] For policy-related purposes, it is perhaps more appropriate to think of *the national interest or the "public interest" as constituting a weighted sum of private interests*. The problem, of course, is how to determine the weights. In a democracy, the weighting of private interests depends on the political process. The "fairness" of that process depends on the access and opportunity that the competing private interests have to present and advocate their respective cases, as well as on the transparency of the process itself.

Winter 1994

Notes

1. Samuel P. Huntington, "America's Changing Strategic Interests," *Survival*, January/February 1991, pp. 8, 15ff.
2. Paul Kennedy, *The Rise and Fall of the Great Powers*, Random House, Inc. 1987, p. 444.
3. Kennedy, 1987, p. 514.
4. John Mueller, *Retreat from Doomsday: The Obsolescence of Major War*, Basic Books, Inc., New York, 1989, p. 221.
5. David Ochmanek, "Foreign Policy Aspects: The Gulf War and Beyond," presented at the RAND Center for U.S.-Japan Relations symposium on "Fairness and Equity in U.S.-Japan Relations," Tokyo, June 21, 1991.
6. In a formal sense, the political and diplomatic instruments can be thought of as other variables, or "shift" variables, that may affect the shape and impact of the economic and military instruments.
7. Alternatively, motivation and volition might be construed as encompassed by the political instruments of power that I mentioned earlier.
8. In symbolic terms, this can be expressed as:

(1) $P_t^q = P(E_t, M_t, X_t)$

where P denotes power, E is a vector of economic instruments, as defined above, M is a vector of military instruments, as defined above, and X is a vector of other variables, including political-diplomatic ones. The index q denotes the state, context, or initial conditions, and t refers to a specified time period.

9. This relationship can be expressed as:

(2) $E_t = E(E_{t-1}, M_t, Y_t)$

where Y is a vector of other relevant variables, and the other terms are as defined in the preceding footnote.

10. This can be stated as:

    (3) $M_t = M(M_{t-1}, E_t Z_t)$

    where Z_t is a vector of other relevant variables.

11. These relationships can be summarized in the following diagram:

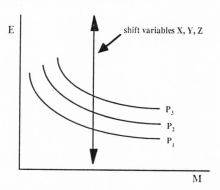

The curves P_1, P_2, P_3 are "isopower" curves showing differing combinations of the economic and military instruments, E and M, respectively, that can be combined to achieve the same level of national power, with $P_3 > P_2 > P_1$. The shift variables x, y, z, can move the isopower curves up or down as indicated by the two-pronged arrow. Strict complementarity between the economic and military instruments would be illustrated by L-shaped isopower curves. In this case, adding more of either instrument would be ineffectual in advancing national power, in the absence of an increment in the other instrument.

12. cf Schumpeter's comment: "There is no scientific sense whatsoever in creating...some metaphysical entity to be called *The Common Good* and a not less metaphysical "state," that, sailing high in the clouds and exempt from and above human struggles and group interests, worships at the shrine of that *Common Good*." (J. A. Schumpeter, "The Communist Manifesto in Sociology and Economics," *Journal of Political Economy*, June 1949, pp. 205–6.)

17

Arms, Trade, and a Less Disorderly World

One enduring aspect of the "old" world order that will seriously complicate as well as influence the emergence of the "new" one is the international market for conventional, but often technologically advanced, arms: aircraft, tanks, artillery, surface-to-air missiles, surface-to-surface missiles, and naval ships. Continuing activity in the arms market will hinder, if not defeat, efforts to sustain stable military balances in various regions of the world and hence to create and maintain a less disorderly world. It is also likely that arms trade may become a delicate issue in the development of improved relations between Russia and the United States—perennially the two largest suppliers in the international arms market.

In the last years of the 1980s decade and the start of the 1990s, the volume of transactions in the international arms market was between $45 billion and $50 billion annually. It is possible that this enormous volume will decrease in the years to come. For example, Iraq's large purchases of arms in the 1980s have been discontinued if not terminated. And the buying power of other third world arms importers will probably be restricted by various factors, including soft prices and reduced earnings from oil exports, competing demands to finance internal economic development, and generally tight conditions in the international capital market.

However, there are other factors that may act in an offsetting direction to sustain a high level of activity in the arms market. On the supply side, these include the growing pressures in the defense industries of the supplier countries to expand exports and thereby partially compensate for diminished domestic procurement. On the demand side, the stimulus will come from the recurrence or emergence of ethnic and irredentist conflicts in the Middle East, Eastern Europe, South Asia, and elsewhere that will boost the demand for weapons by potential buyers.

In recent years, the former Soviet Union was the largest seller with about 40 percent, or $20 billion, in worldwide sales. Only a third of this amount, about $6 billion annually, represented hard currency sales—the remainder was typically financed by soft, long-term ruble loans which have been and are likely to remain largely unrequited. Still, even at this level, arms exports have been the second largest source of hard currency earnings of the former Soviet economy, exceeded only by export earnings from oil and natural gas. The United States has been the second largest seller with about 20 percent of the global total, or $10 to 11 billion annually.

In October 1991, the five principal arms suppliers (the so-called "first-tier" suppliers)—France, China, the United Kingdom, the United States, and the then-Soviet Union, now principally Russia—agreed upon a nonbinding arms trade protocol. The agreement provides for the maintenance of a current registry with full information about arms exports by the G-5 suppliers, as well as for serious efforts to restrain this trade. Specifically, the signatories have agreed to avoid weapons transfers that would "aggravate an existing armed conflict...increase tension...or introduce destabilizing military capabilities." Aside from its other limitations—notably, its nonbinding character, and its emphasis on good intentions rather than enforcement mechanisms—the October protocol is impaired by its failure to consider the so-called "second-tier" arms suppliers, notably Brazil, India, Israel, North and South Korea, as well as others. Restraint by the main suppliers, should it occur as a result of the October protocol, may actually encourage rather than discourage the second-tier suppliers to fill the breach.

The ensuing competition may be further abetted by potential arms importers in the Middle East and elsewhere. In the absence of effective means of stabilizing regional military balances, potential arms buyers in the Middle East and elsewhere may actively seek arms imports from second-tier suppliers to substitute for weapons systems that may become harder to obtain from first-tier suppliers.

There are still other considerations that make this entire scene even more worrisome. As the U.S. defense budget declines, spending on procurement, which has typically been about 30 to 35 percent of total defense spending, is likely to be under particularly severe constraints. As a result of recently announced policy changes by the Department of Defense, more emphasis is to be placed in future defense budgets on research, development, test, and evaluation (RDT&E), and less on procurement, with a view to building so-called "shelf" capabilities, rather than deployed ones. Where procurement orders are placed, they are likely to be for relatively small production runs. As a consequence of these new policies, stronger incentives will be created for defense industry firms to look toward sales abroad as a means of defraying the fixed costs of development and the smaller production runs at home. As mentioned earlier, similar pressures impend in the other principal supplier countries, with the result that arms producers are likely to devote increased efforts to stimulating the demand for their exports, as well as to obtain government subsidies for them.

These circumstances present particularly complex choices and challenges for Russia, and to a lesser extent Ukraine and Kazakhstan, as the principal arms producers of the former Soviet Union. U.S. policy toward these republics of the Commonwealth of Independent States is likely to confront awkward dilemmas relating to arms trade issues. As President Yeltsin pursues his strong efforts to marketize the Russian economy, the plain fact is that weapons production is a sector in which Russia can be presumed to have a comparative advantage relative to other potential export sectors. As noted earlier, arms exports have perennially been the former Soviet Union's second largest source of hard-currency earnings. Consequently, U.S. policy may confront a choice in either of two directions, both of which are awkward and risky. One choice would be simply to raise no objection to Russian competition in the international arms market, with the expectation that higher-performance American weapons will predominate in the marketplace, as they did against Soviet equipment fielded by Iraq in Desert Storm. However, while American suppliers in the arms market may now feel confident that their established clients in the Middle East and elsewhere will continue to prefer American jet aircraft, ships, tanks, and air defense and strike missiles to Russian varieties, the progress of marketization in Russia may make the Russian brands quite competitive on cost and quantity grounds in the future.

The other direction for American policy is to endorse and try to enforce binding limitations on global arms trade, in the process incurring political opposition from our own afflicted defense industrial firms, as well as breaches and evasions by firms and governments of the other supplier countries.

The first choice—competition among arms sellers abroad, especially Russia and other first- and second-tier sellers—will add fuel to the fires of instability that smolder in various regions of the disorderly world. The second choice—undertaking serious efforts to establish, monitor, and enforce vigorous collective controls over arms exports and imports— will face serious political opposition at home and abroad, as well as considerable risk of failure because of the powerful incentives that will be operating in both exporting and importing countries to expand the arms trade, regardless of formal agreements.

For the "new world order" to have a chance of being less disorderly than the one it supersedes, the second course of action is the more promising road to travel.

There is also an important self-interested reason for endorsing this second approach. With dissolution of the Soviet Union, the United States faces few if any adversaries with the capability to provide their own military equipment. Very few nations have that capability. Rather, adversaries that the U.S. may encounter in possible future regional conflicts will depend almost entirely on the international weapons market to meet their needs. Hence, control or regulation of that market offers the possibility of significantly limiting the extent to which there are nations capable of posing threats to vital U.S. interests. For this reason, too, developing mechanisms for such control and regulation should be an important component of U.S. strategy for the new world order.

March 1992

18

Gun Control at Home, Decontrol Abroad

Although U.S. domestic policies are trying to restrict sales of relatively small, "old-tech" weapons at home (through the Brady Law, the impending ban on assault weapons, and other gun control measures), it is ironic that U.S. foreign and defense policies are expanding sales of large, "high-tech" weapons abroad.

While gun control at home may contribute to improved domestic security, increased foreign sales of advanced weapons create serious hazards for security and stability abroad.

In the late 1980s, the United States' share of the then $55 billion international weapons market was less than that of the Soviet Union (about 25 percent compared to the Soviet Union's 40 percent), while the remaining sales were made by France, China, Britain, and other suppliers. It might have been expected that the weapons market would decrease sharply in the 1990s due both to the end of the cold war and financial constraints faced by third world buyers. In fact, the market is close to its previous peak—it is currently over $50 billion annually—as a result of price-cutting and eased financing from suppliers, as well as larger-than-expected demands by buyers in the Middle East, South Asia, and East Asia.

The United States has become by far the largest weapon supplier— over 60 percent of the current market—with the remainder divided among Russia, China, France, and others. These weapon sales—including advanced fighter aircraft, missiles, armed helicopters, radars, improved munitions, and naval vessels—will substantially raise the level of violence in future regional conflicts and in international peacekeeping efforts in which American military forces may be involved.

Three principal reasons underlie the expanded role of U.S. weapons sales. First, improving the defense capabilities of countries friendly to the United States—notably, Israel, Egypt, Korea, Saudi Arabia, Taiwan, Turkey, Greece, Indonesia, among others—may, in the disorderly post-cold war environment, enhance regional order and stability by making these countries less vulnerable to aggression against them, thereby reducing the probability of regional conflicts.

Second, third world buyers generally prefer U.S. weapons because their technical performance and cost characteristics are superior to the systems provided by other potential suppliers. The weapons market is working as markets are supposed to work: better producers acquire larger market shares.

Third, arms exports provide a partial offset to the severe cutbacks in U.S. defense procurement, and thus a means of keeping the U.S. defense industrial base from eroding too rapidly.

For those who remain concerned and unconvinced by the logic or the validity of these propositions, there is a decisive additional reason that condones expansion of the U.S. share of the global arms market. If U.S. firms were to forgo opportunities for increasing sales abroad, other suppliers—especially France, Russia, China, and Britain—would simply rush in to fill the breach.

The result is that international weapons proliferation proceeds in a relatively unchecked way, thereby storing up serious security problems for the future by ignoring them in the present.

There is a better approach.

As a practical matter, the arms trade cannot be terminated, but it can be selectively controlled. The essence of a practicable control regime is to focus prospective controls on only those weapons whose proliferation would seriously destabilize regional arms balances. These balances could become unstable if arms imports were to alter significantly the existing balance of military forces among countries within, say, the Middle East or East Asian regions, or if such imports made it substantially more difficult for forces from outside the region to be brought to bear to maintain the force balance within the region. The result would be to diminish the effectiveness of external forces as a deterrent to aggression within the region. "High-leverage" weapon systems, that would have such effects, can be separately identified among the much larger set of total arms sales in the global market. For example, high-leverage systems include missiles, advanced munitions, submarines, radar-absorbing platforms, and advanced sea and land mines.

Fortunately, such high-leverage systems constitute a relatively small proportion—perhaps only 10 percent of the global weapons market; most weapons sales are for air and naval platforms (aircraft and naval vessels), tanks, armed vehicles, artillery, and communications. So, prohibiting the sale of high-leverage systems would impose only a modest financial loss on the major suppliers, specifically, on the U.S. as well as Russia, China, France, and Britain.

Developing such a selective control system would require agreement among the "big five" suppliers—the United States, Russia, China, France, and Britain—to establish a joint "market stabilizing mechanism." The proposed MSM would enforce prohibition against only the sales of specific high-leverage weapons through a system of penalties and rewards that has been developed and described in recent and ongoing work at RAND. To be sure, implementation of such a control regime would pose a formidable challenge to international negotiation among the five principal suppliers, but the task is both practicable and overdue. Accomplishing it is vastly preferable to the present myopic policy of allowing the weapons market to proceed in an unchecked manner at the cost of grievous problems in the not-too-distant future.

June 1994

19

Nixon's View of the World

If a contest were held for the best extended essay on the state of the world by a living former president of the United States, Richard Nixon's *Seize the Moment: America's Challenge in a One-Superpower World* (Simon & Schuster) would win the prize.

If eligibility were extended to allow participation by former heads of government in other countries, Nixon's book would still be a good bet, but entries by Margaret Thatcher, Helmut Schmidt, and Yasuhiro Nakasone would make the contest closer and more interesting.

Seize the Moment is a *tour d'horizon* of global scope that addresses the current state of the world, where it is heading, and the challenge that these trends portend for U.S. interests and policies. It also presents a challenge to an author who aspires to describe it and prescribe policies that the "one superpower" should follow—a challenge that Nixon meets confidently and competently. That the book's coverage is uneven—generally better in sketching the big picture than the fine-grained details—is not surprising. One might hope that the country does as well in actually meeting the challenges it faces as Nixon does in prescribing for them.

Nixon's ninth book (eight have been published since he left the White House in 1974) begins with an overview chapter on "The Real World"—a title presumably intended as a contrast to the mythological world inhabited by many foreign policy commentators. Nixon takes careful aim at "three myths that [have] dominated the debate about the future of U.S. foreign policy." The first is the "myth of the end of history." (In Nixon's view, the reality is that it is quite premature to proclaim "the triumph of...liberal democracy and market economics.") The second is the "myth of the irrelevance of military power." (In reality, "those who propound the irrelevance of military power vastly overstate the influence of economic power.") And the third is the "myth of the decline of America," in contrast to the reality that the United States is "the only country that possesses global economic, military, and political power."

The second and longest chapter deals with "The Former Evil Empire," a subject to which Nixon brings insight as well as experience. His evaluations of Gorbachev ("a Soviet version of Adlai Stevenson") and Yeltsin ("a combination of John Wayne and Lyndon Johnson") are acute, especially so since they were made in September 1991, four months before Gorbachev's resignation as president of the since-dissolved Soviet Union. Nixon forecasts a future in which the republics of the former Soviet Union can be "not only allies, but also friends" of the United States. Toward this end, he calls for direct ties to the republics, strong support for Yeltsin's efforts at comprehensive systemic economic reform, but avoidance of Marshall Plan-type financial assistance. "The greatest contribution the United States could make," he concludes, is "not financial, but ideological."

Seize the Moment then addresses successively Europe ("The Common Transatlantic Home"), "The Pacific Triangle" (China, Japan, Russia), "The Muslim World," the less-developed countries ("The Southern Hemisphere"), and "The Renewal of America." Although for the most part his broad-brush treatment is sound and well-informed, Nixon's literary style is at times cloyingly didactic and categoric. Besides the "three myths," there are "three dangers" (that "could make the victory of freedom short-lived"), "three fundamental errors," "four fundamental geopolitical facts," "five new realities," "three basic currents of Muslim thought," "three fatal illusions," and "five basic rules" for U.S. policy in the Arab-Israeli dispute!

In the course of Nixon's tour of the world scene, he endorses comprehensive and rapid transformation of the former Soviet republics' economies ("broader implementation of the Polish 'shock therapy' model"), rather than piecemeal gradualism. Advocates of "democratic socialism"— whether in the former Soviet Union or in the West—are a frequent target of Nixon's severe criticism. He sees, but perhaps underestimates, the rising tide of protectionism in the European Community, but concludes that "the strategic benefits [of European integration] continue to outweigh the economic costs of rising protectionism." Nixon makes a novel suggestion for how the United States might circumvent this protectionist EC trend. He proposes a two-step process in which the EC grants associate-member status to the East European countries, while the United

States forges "a close economic relationship" with them that could "give the United States a potential backdoor into an increasingly protectionist post-1992 Europe."

Turning to Japan, Nixon repeats much that is familiar in recent discussion of U.S.-Japanese economic and political relations. He is neither a "basher" nor an apologist for Japanese mercantilism, urging that "we should not fear but learn from competition." Nevertheless, he would accept, but "only as a last resort...selective retaliation if the Japanese refuse to abandon clear and identifiable unfair trade practices."

Nixon's discussion of China and its old-guard leadership is balanced as well as forthright. While favoring increased U.S. economic "engagement" with China, he proposes that we foster political change not only by resuming "high-level dialogue" with the Chinese leadership, but also by opening up two new broadcast stations, Radio Free China, and Radio Free Tibet, "to provide these nations with independent information and commentary." He also proposes condign toughness in resisting and penalizing foreign sales by China of nuclear technologies and missiles, while urging that the United States should "enhance Taiwan's international political standing."

The book's treatment of "The Muslim World" is particularly uneven. For example, he asserts that the "electoral appeal [of fundamentalism] is weak"—a judgment that seems highly questionable in light of the recent Algerian election returns. And he dismisses efforts at regional arms control in the Middle East as both "inadvisable" and "unfeasible," although the reasons he offers to sustain this judgment are arguable, if not wrong.

Turning to "The Southern Hemisphere," Nixon argues for measured U.S. concern and involvement for moral, economic, and security reasons. He excoriates the statist propensities of "Western academics," and strongly and unsurprisingly endorses free markets, human capital investment, limited government tax burdens, foreign investment, and export-led growth as the policy directions that the United States should encourage in the developing world. He is less convinced than many that "democracy is the answer to the underdeveloped world's problems," citing the experience of the four Asian "tigers" as grounds for his doubts.

The concluding chapter of *Seize the Moment* addresses the "renewal of America," providing the usual list of the country's problems—savings, investment, education, crime, drugs, the homeless, and so on. This discussion is longer on rhetoric than it is on solutions. He argues that "birthright entitlements [are] corroding American society," suggesting further that solutions lie in the realm of "values, attitudes, and behavior," and that these are not dependent on dollars.

Nixon concludes with a call for American leadership in a period fraught with opportunities as well as dangers. He endorses for the present era Winston Churchill's statement of forty-five years ago that "the United States stands...at the pinnacle of world power...with primacy in power is also joined an awe-inspiring accountability for the future." And Nixon concludes that, "We must seize the moment not just for ourselves but for others."

If Nixon's book is at times as much sermon as it is analysis, he has the fundamentals right. His generally upbeat attitude toward America's opportunities and capabilities provides a refreshing contrast to the "nattering negativism" that abounds in many recent pronouncements by members of the community of foreign policy experts.

February 1992

20

Where the Disorderly World is Heading

Since the start of the post-cold war era, policymakers, professors, and pundits have been searching for a suitable vocabulary to describe it.

One formulation proposed by the Bush Administration, referred to the "New World Order"—terminology that was somewhat odious because the same words had been used by Hitler to describe where he thought he was heading. Another formulation, favored by Jeffrey Garten, Jacques Attali, and others, depicts the new world situation as one dominated by three economic rivals: the United States, the European Community, and Japan. Still another focused on the decreasing role of military power and its ceding of precedence to economic power—a formulation favored by Samuel Huntington and others.

Max Singer and Aaron Wildavsky propose another, more encompassing and cogent formulation in *The* Real *World Order: Zones of Peace/ Zones of Turmoil* (Chatham House Publishers).

Singer, sometime head of the Hudson Institute (to whose founder, Herman Kahn, the book is dedicated), and Wildavsky, a Berkeley political science professor, conceive of the "*real* world order" as consisting of two fundamentally separable, but interacting, parts: the "zones of peace," and the "zones of turmoil." The zones of peace consist of Western Europe, the U.S., Canada, Japan, and the Antipodes. All are democracies, and according to Singer and Wildavsky, their quintessential but often overlooked attribute is that "modern democracies do not go to war with one another, do not even seriously imagine the possibility of being at war with one another." Singer and Wildavsky acknowledge that there will be disagreements and conflicts among members of the zones of peace, including conflicts over their differing concerns in the zones of turmoil. However, in the world situation that impends, countries in the zones of peace will not "be divided into competing military blocs seeking to balance each other's power," nor will "the political relations among (these) countries...be influenced by relative military power." Consequently, the "real world order" in the zones of peace "will be fundamentally different from any past world order"—a point the authors believe "that most academics and diplomats have so far failed to grasp."

However, the zones of peace contain only 15 percent of the world's population. The remaining 85 percent lives in the zones of turmoil, which Singer and Wildavsky characterize as "an immense, slowly boiling cauldron, agitated by powerful internal forces that are impossible to control...where poverty, war, tyranny, and anarchy will continue to devastate lives." Singer and Wildavsky do not imply that the zones of turmoil are undifferentiated or unchanging. They acknowledge that several new democracies have emerged there, observing that the "difficult processes of economic and political development...will cause wealth, democracy and peace gradually to spread through these zones." However, their view of gradualism envisages 100 to 200 years for the spread to be extensive.

In elaborating and applying their paradigm, Singer and Wildavsky advance many valid and provocative, as well as arguable, propositions. These propositions, together with my assessment of their validity, include the following:

- Military force will be, "the ultimate determinant of what happens in the zones of turmoil" (valid, but exaggerated).
- In these zones, "the transition from...poverty to...wealth...is almost inevitable almost everywhere" (probably wrong), but "the transition to democracy is weaker and more tentative" (probably valid).
- Acquisition of nuclear weapons, as well as chemical and biological weapons, will be attractive to countries in the zones of turmoil because, "the democracies will be reluctant to intervene in conflicts in the zones of turmoil, against a country armed with nuclear weapons" (valid).
- With respect to intervention in the zones of turmoil, Singer and Wildavsky make a critical distinction between "objectives" that we are potentially willing to use military force to achieve, and "principles" that reflect "what we believe in." They urge that the principles should be "ambitious" while the objectives should be limited—and hence our interventions should also be limited and selective (valid).
- In the zones of turmoil, "The United States has no geopolitical or strategic interests...important enough to dominate our policy." Consequently, "our policy—outside of economics—should be to support principles...chosen to

try to make the international order somewhat more civilized, primarily by developing and enforcing traditional international law" (perhaps valid, surely arguable).

Singer and Wildavsky demur from much of the conventional wisdom about Russia and the former Soviet Union, which they place in the zones of turmoil. They assert that, "The United States does not have enough wisdom or power to have much chance of being able to have a positive influence on the survival of stable government in Russia…(because) the forces at work there are too strong." Moreover, "While chaos in Russia is not without risk,…it is not a major threat to the United States…nor will any plausible outcome in Russia produce a dangerous threat to western Europe," notwithstanding the 30,000 nuclear weapons in the territory of the former Soviet Union. Those who argue "that American national security depends on preserving stability in Russia," according to Singer and Wildavsky, exaggerate what U.S. policy can possibly achieve there, and in the process "lose objectivity, credibility, and bargaining power without significantly increasing the chance of achieving our objective." Instead, Singer and Wildavsky suggest that we should assume that instability "is reasonably likely and do what we can to protect ourselves against its dangers."

The authors conclude that "peace in the zones of democracy is compatible with war in the zones of turmoil." Contrary to the standard shibboleth that "peace is indivisible," they contend that "the divisibility of peace is one of the fundamental advantages of the current world order."

The Real *World Order* provides an original and provocative contribution to reflection and debate about the extraordinary era that is upon us. Unfortunately, the book's merit and message are marred by too much first-draft prose and careless editing. One example among many: in discussing Russia's predicament, Singer and Wildavsky say that ,"No hope can be expected from no economy."

August 1993

Part III

The Economies of Japan and China

21

Dissecting the Japanese Problem with "Occam's Razor"

Six hundred years ago, an English cleric, William of Occam, proposed a fundamental principle to guide philosophic inquiry. Subsequently called "Occam's razor," the principle stipulates that simple explanations and answers should be preferred to complex ones; complexities should only be introduced when simple explanations have been proven inadequate.

Occam's razor is also helpful in nonphilosophical realms. For example, it can be usefully applied to answer the familiar and troublesome questions about the performance and competitiveness of the Japanese economy: its relatively rapid growth, its aggressive development of high-technology industry, its large and continuing export surpluses, and the economic "threat" it is said to pose to U.S. "competitiveness."

All of these issues can be understood and accounted for by simple explanations without recourse to the more complex ones invoked by such commentators as Chalmers Johnson, Karel Van Wolferen, James Fallows, Clyde Prestowitz, and Pat Choate in expressing their often strident criticism of Japanese policy and urging adoption of a countervailing American one. The targets of their criticism include Japan's industrial policy, the special role of MITI, the prevalence of collusive Japanese business practices, keiretsu industrial organizations, tariff and nontariff trade barriers, discriminatory regulatory and contractual practices, and finally, Japanese culture and society.

Notwithstanding that there is some truth in these allegations, most of the explanation for Japan's formidable economic record and challenge lies elsewhere. It lies in four simple, dominant, and straightforward facts, some of which are likely to be transitory.

The first is Japan's high rate of aggregate domestic investment—averaging about 24 percent of its GNP in the late 1980s, compared to a rate of about 16 percent in the United States.

The second is Japan's still higher rate of domestic savings—averaging about 28 percent of its GNP in the late 1980s, compared to a figure of only 13 or 14 percent in the United States.

The third contributing factor is a highly disciplined, trained, industrious, and literate Japanese labor force. And the fourth is an energetic, competent, and experienced management that has learned, through exposure to intense domestic and international competition, to strive continually to raise product quality and cut production costs.

The first of the four facts accounts for nearly all of the difference in average annual growth rates—about 2 or 3 percentage points—between Japan and the United States. It also largely explains Japan's particularly strong performance in certain specific sectors—for example, automobiles, consumer electronics and semiconductors—which are capital-intensive or R&D-intensive.

The first and second facts, taken together, account for Japan's persistent trade surpluses (which are explained by the excess of its domestic savings over its domestic investment rate); they also account for the persistent trade deficits of the United States (the excess of its domestic investment over domestic savings).

And the third and fourth factors account for Japan's generally more rapid growth of productivity—although this is more arguable than the preceding inferences.

In the next five years, Japan's savings rate is likely to fall somewhat as a result of rising consumer demands and a population whose proportion of elderly people is increasing more rapidly than that of the United States and other industrialized countries. Japan's investment rate may also decrease as a result of tighter capital markets and a reallocation of resources from the private to the public sector. For similar reasons, Japan's productivity growth will probably also decrease in this time period.

It is difficult for the United States to boost its savings rate, but tax policies provide one means of doing so: for example, by allowing for partial deductibiity of interest income, while reducing the tax deductibility of interest payments. If the United States wants to raise its investment rate, reduction of capital gains taxation would also be warranted—although here too, political feasibility and economic desirability collide.

These comments do not invalidate the complaints and criticisms that have been made by the critics mentioned earlier. Nor does it follow that the United States should forgo applying strong and persistent pressure, through Super 301 and other means, to level Japan's economic "playing field."

For example, it is increasingly inappropriate and aggravating that Japanese restrictions impede efforts by American firms to establish manufacturing plants in Osaka or Nagoya, or that formal and informal restrictions prevent foreign firms from trading on the Tokyo stock exchange, or that American engineering and construction firms should find innumerable, often subtle obstacles placed in the way of submitting competing bids and being fairly judged in contract awards. And it is anachronistic for the Japanese to invoke the outmoded shibboleth of "food security" to justify their opposition to agricultural trade liberalization through GATT.

Persistence of these practices is galling to the American public and the Congress, demeans Japan's international standing, and harms the broad relationship between the United States and Japan. Like the spectacle of tax-cheating by the rich, beggaring one's neighbor is especially offensive when practiced by those who are economically strong. However, application of Occam's razor suggests that such objectionable practices probably account for a very small part of Japan's impressive economic accomplishments and its prominent and powerful position in the world economy.

May 1991

22

Resuming the Protracted U.S.-Japan Economic Debate

Whether the perennial economic negotiations between the United States and Japan are advertised as a "Structural Impediments Initiative" as in the 1980s, or as a "Strategic Trade Policy" initiative as in the present, the accompanying dialogue follows a similarly ritualistic pattern. According to the ritual, the Americans begin and conclude by vigorously asserting that the fundamental problem (of Japan's chronic and large trade surplus with the United States) is Japan's closed markets, and the obvious remedy is to open them. The Japanese start and conclude by no less vigorously asserting that the real culprit is the large U.S. budget deficit, and the obvious remedy is to eliminate it by raising taxes.

In fact, neither side has much going for it. The American contention is accurate but largely irrelevant, while that of the Japanese is simply wrong. Moreover, a departure from the ritual could provide a way of both reducing the chronic Japanese surplus and turning the Japanese economy around from its currently serious recession.

The American stance in the standard ritual is irrelevant because, while Japan's domestic markets are demonstrably less permeable than markets elsewhere, the U.S. current account deficit—covering both merchandise and services trade with Japan as well as with the rest of the world—does not result from that fact. It results from, and is exactly equal to, the amount by which U.S. gross domestic saving falls short of U.S. gross domestic investment. Consequently, the global U.S. current account deficit—about 90 billion dollars in 1993, over half of which was with Japan—won't be significantly affected by the opening of Japan's markets, although such a move is long overdue to improve the well-being of Japan's short-changed consumers and taxpayers, and to help in adjusting Japan's mercantilist vestiges to the new GATT world.

The Japanese position has more serious flaws than the American one.

The first flaw is empirical: The link that the Japanese assert between the two deficits doesn't exist! As the accompanying graphic shows, in the period since the mid-1980s, the budget deficit and the current account deficit have been uncorrelated with one another. The two deficits moved in opposite directions more often (five years) than they moved in the same direction (two years).

Although the two deficits have sometimes been referred to as "twins," they are, at most, third-cousins!

Second, the Japanese refrain is also weak on theoretical grounds. Establishing a causal link between budget deficits and current account defi-

FIGURE 22.1
U.S. Economic Indicators
(billions of dollars)

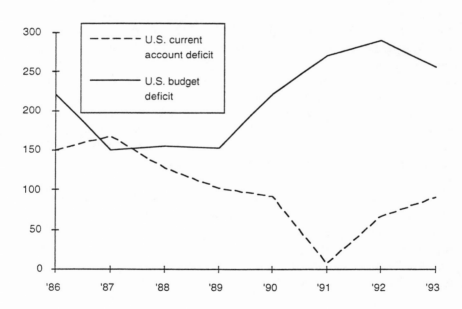

cits involves a questionable chain of reasoning. On the one hand, government borrowing (to finance budget deficits) is supposed to correspondingly deplete private savings, thereby *increasing* the imbalance between domestic savings and investment and hence raising the U.S. current account deficit. On the other hand, government borrowing also raises interest rates and "crowds out" private investment, thereby *reducing* the imbalance between savings and investment, and presumably lowering the current account deficit. How these complex and offsetting effects net out is neither clear nor well understood, and does not warrant the standard admonition usually imparted by the Japanese to their American interlocutors that cutting the U.S. budget deficit would cure the trade deficit.

Third, the Japanese emphasis on the causal effect of the U.S. budget deficit carries with it mistaken implications for policy. The usual policy inference is that eliminating or at least reducing the budget deficit will equivalently affect the global current account imbalance of the United States, as well as that vis-à-vis Japan. But this inference is wrong. The U.S. current account deficit can be closed or reduced if and only if gross saving in the U.S. is increased, or gross investment is decreased, or saving rises by more than investment, so the gap between them narrows. If the budget deficit is reduced by fiscal policies that increase taxes on high-saving, corporate and individual income recipients, there will be little or no effect on the current account deficit, because revenues raised from these sources will simply reduce the savings that would otherwise have occurred. Hence, the savings-investment imbalance won't be changed, and the current account deficit won't be reduced.

Finally, it is worth reminding Japanese policy makers and the influential bureaucracies in the Ministries of Finance, Foreign Affairs, and Trade and Industry, that the U.S. savings–investment imbalance is neither more or less culpable than is Japan's corresponding but opposite imbalance. The excess of Japan's domestic savings over its domestic investment is the mirror image of the U.S. shortfall of savings over its domestic investment, and this excess is the fundamental source of Japan's chronic export surpluses.

Japan's failure to recognize this fact is unfortunately reflected by the new fiscal policies currently under discussion by the Hosokawa government in Tokyo. These policies call for lowering marginal income tax rates (a sensible as well as overdue measure), but retaining and perhaps even increasing the existing tax on consumption (clearly inappropriate, under the circumstances). Were Japan genuinely to seek to remedy, or at least mitigate, its global current account surplus, as well as that with the United States, it would combine lower income taxes with *removal* of the present tax on consumption, while taxing private savings that have long been treated as nontaxable income. Moreover, this set of policies is precisely what is needed to reverse Japan's economic recession by increasing disposable income and domestic spending, as well as Japan's imports from the United States and the rest of the world. Such a departure by the Japanese from the standard U.S.-Japan economic ritual would thus contribute both to reducing Japan's chronic external surplus *and* turning its domestic economy around.

U.S. negotiators would be well-advised to place more emphasis on such improvements in Japan's macroeconomic policies, rather than only trying to open Japan's protected markets by seeking to "manage" them.

January 1994

23

Clearing the Fog Over U.S.-Japan
Economic Relations

Whether the current upheaval in Japanese politics will affect its economies for good or ill is unclear. If the political reformers like Mr. Hata and
Mr. Ozawa are more concerned than their predecessors with the lot of
Japanese consumers and taxpayers, the effect should be salutary. It's
more doubtful that the effect will please America's most vehement critics
of Japan's trade policy because their expectations are misconceived.

Japanese consumers and taxpayers would surely benefit, and American exporters would perhaps benefit, if Japan opened its markets more
fully, eliminated its often subtle nontariff barriers to imports of services
as well as goods, and removed existing restrictions on participation by
foreign firms in Japanese government procurement contracts. That the
benefits realized by American exporters would be less assured than those
realized by Japanese consumers is due to the fact that other Asian and
European exporters would doubtless share in the increased sales to Japan.

While these measures might have some effect in reducing the bilateral
U.S. deficit in merchandise trade with Japan, they would have no effect
on the more significant global U.S. current account deficit—the excess
of U.S. payments for all imports of goods and services over its earnings
from exports of goods and services. This deficit, currently running at an
annual rate of about $50 billion, represents the difference between the
U.S. global deficit of $110 billion in merchandise trade (half of which is
with Japan), and the U.S. global surplus of $60 billion in services trade
(of which about $10 billion is with Japan).

The $50 billion current account deficit will not be affected by liberal-
ization of the Japanese market because that deficit depends on, and is
exactly equal to, the amount by which gross savings in the U.S. fall short
of gross investment in the U.S.—a difference of almost 1 percent of the

U.S. gross domestic product. In its turn, the savings versus investment deficit depends on U.S. macroeconomic policies—specifically on U.S. fiscal and monetary policies—not on the residual vestiges of Japanese mercantilism reflected in its protective trade policies.

Being "tough" in trade negotiations with Japan, as a reflection of what is sometimes referred to as "strategic trade policy," or "managed trade," may or may not affect Japan's willingness to adopt the liberalization measures mentioned above. But, whether the result is Japanese accommodation or, what is equally likely, Japanese resistance, the U.S. current account deficit will not be affected—a point that has been virtually ignored in most official as well as press discussions of the subject.

Absent a rise in U.S. savings, or a fall in U.S. investment, increased U.S. exports to Japan will simply lead to increased U.S. imports from Japan or elsewhere, or reductions in other U.S. exports, without changing the overall U.S. current account deficit. Expectations to the contrary will inevitably be disappointed, resulting in scapegoating and resentment in both the U.S. and Japan. In the U.S., Japan will be blamed, however much or little it concedes, because shrinking the U.S. current account deficit depends on measures that are largely unrelated to whatever Japan does or refrains from doing on trade liberalization. In Japan, the U.S. will be blamed for unrealistically expecting from Japan what depends instead on macroeconomic conditions and policies in the U.S.

The recalcitrant U.S. current account deficit might be reduced by a rise in U.S. gross savings, or a fall in U.S. gross investment. Either or both of these might come about as a result of a serious recession—clearly something that would be much less welcome than the current account deficit—or by further depreciation of the already undervalued dollar, which might increase gross savings as a result of worsening the terms of trade. They might preferably come about through reductions in government spending or changes in the U.S. tax structure that could raise both savings and investment while reducing the difference between them.

Much of the foregoing is controversial. None of it should be, because it follows inescapably from the facts of the matter. That this misunderstanding is so widespread, reflects the deplorable gap between rhetoric and perceptions, on the one hand, and reality, on the other.

The gap between rhetoric and reality contributed to the acerbic tone of the last meeting in Washington between President Clinton and Prime Minister Miyazawa in April. It may also mar the forthcoming July 7th summit meeting of the G-7 heads of government in Tokyo because international trade will be one of the two main items on the meeting's agenda (the other is aid to Russia). What Mike Mansfield, the former U.S. Ambassador to Japan, referred to as "the most important bilateral relationship in the world, bar none," would be less troubled in the future than it currently is if this gap between rhetoric and reality were diminished—not only between the U.S. and Japan, but within the U.S. government as well.

July 1993

24

The Strong Yen of a Weakened Economy

Paradoxically, the recent strength of the Japanese yen relative to the U.S. dollar is a reflection of the *weakened* Japanese economy—specifically, the depth and duration of its recession—rather than its strength! The weakness of the U.S. dollar—its depreciation relative to the yen—carries with it little implication or significance with respect to the underlying health of the U.S. economy or its prospects for sustained growth.

At the start of 1994, when the yen value of the dollar was 110, a reasonably convincing case could be made—and indeed was endorsed by various international financial mavens including George Soros—that the dollar's foreign exchange value was likely to rise in the coming months. That case was based on six plausible reasons:

- Growth of the U.S. economy was faster than that of Japan and Western Europe—3 percent faster than that of Japan, and 2 to 3 percent faster than that of Germany.
- The recent growth in U.S. productivity, both in services and manufacturing, was among the highest in the industrialized world.
- Wage increases were moderate or flat, so U.S. real labor costs were relatively low.
- U.S. corporate profits were rising relative to those elsewhere.
- The U.S. price level was stable—the annual rate of growth in the CPI was about 2 percent, and of the PPI, about 1 percent.
- The real purchasing power of the dollar at home was more than 40 percent above that of the yen or the mark, as U.S. travelers to those countries knew well.

The first four reasons provided incentives for foreign investment in the U.S.—especially foreign direct investment and investment in equities—to rise. Hence, increased foreign demand for dollars from this source would tend to boost the exchange value of the dollar. Similarly, several of the reasons—productivity growth, low real labor costs, stable prices, and the dollar's relatively high purchasing power—warranted a forecast that U.S. international competitiveness would be strong and exports would rise, adding to foreign demand for dollars, and tending to boost further the dollar's exchange value.

While the case for expecting appreciation of the dollar was entirely plausible, what actually happened was quite different, as well as more complex. Instead of appreciation, a substantial depreciation of about 10 percent has occurred in the dollar's value relative to the yen, and a somewhat smaller drop in the dollar's value relative to the mark. At the same time, there has been a slight *rise* in the U.S. dollar's exchange value relative to the Canadian dollar and the Mexican peso—currencies of two of the three principal trading partners of the United States. Netting all of these changes, the result has been a 2 or 3 percent depreciation of the dollar relative to all foreign currencies on a trade-weighted basis.

A convincing explanation for the substantial depreciation of the dollar relative to the yen lies in the unexpected length and depth of the Japanese recession. Thus, the strength of the yen is the direct result of the weakness of the Japanese economy, not its strength!

The liquidity of Japanese financial and nonfinancial businesses has been severely stressed in recent months by two factors: first, the slump in corporate profits of nonfinancial businesses, and second, the pressure on balance sheets and income statements of financial businesses due to actual and potential marking down of their nonperforming loans. Underlying the pressure on these balance sheets has been the sharp fall in property values in the past few years following collapse of the "bubble economy," as well as the very limited recovery in the asset value of corporate equities cross-held by Japanese financial institutions. As a result, several large mortgage-financing companies have filed for bankruptcy within the last year, and some of Japan's major money center banks have been obliged to make increasing—though still insufficient—provisions for loss reserves to cover their bad debts.

To relieve this liquidity crunch at home, Japanese financial and nonfinancial businesses have been reducing their large holdings of dollar assets—including U.S. equities, real property, and government bonds and converting the dollar proceeds to yen.

Furthermore, Japan's economic growth in 1994 has been a full percentage point below what was anticipated—hovering between 0.5 percent positive growth and 0.5 percent negative growth—resulting in a probable decrease in Japanese imports in 1994 relative to 1993. The low level of imports has reduced Japanese demand for dollars, while swelling Japan's current account surplus with the U.S. to an estimated $80 billion in 1994 compared to $60 billion in 1993.

Thus, depreciation of the dollar has principally been due to the increased supply of dollars resulting from liquidation of dollar assets referred to earlier, and reduced Japanese demand for dollars resulting from lagging growth of the Japanese economy and decreasing imports.

The bottom line is that the reasonable grounds existing at the start of 1994 for expecting the dollar to appreciate have been overwhelmed by factors associated with the continued weakness of the Japanese economy.

Since the principal explanation for the strengthened yen lies in the depth and duration of Japan's recession, the principal remedies lie in the purview of Japanese policy makers, not in that of the Federal Reserve Board. These remedies include reducing Japan's tax rates, removing its consumption tax, increasing public works expenditures, and easing credit policy. With even a modest dose of these remedies, a substantial appreciation of the dollar's value relative to the yen can be expected in the not-distant future.

July 1994

25

Sense and Nonsense About Dealing with Japan

Japan consumes and invests domestically *less* than it produces—by an amount that is about 3 percent of its gross domestic product. The United States consumes and invests domestically *more* than it produces—by an amount that is about 1.75 percent of its GDP. As long as these respective imbalances persist, the U.S. will have a *deficit* and Japan will have a *surplus* in their respective international current accounts. Getting "tough" over Japan's imports of cars and auto parts may make U.S. policymakers feel good, but will not alter these imbalances. If the two countries' corresponding surpluses and deficits are not incurred with one another, they'll be incurred with other trading partners.

None of this condones Japan's continued mercantilism, and its anachronistic nontariff and distributional impediments to opening its markets to imports of cars, auto parts, telecommunications, medical equipment, financial services, and government procurement. Nor does this indictment gainsay the fact that Japan has already made efforts and progress—however slow and insufficient—toward opening its markets to foreign products and services.

However, if either the U.S. or Japan really wants to alter their respective and opposite imbalances, there are better and worse ways of going about it. Applying sanctions to Japanese auto exports to the U.S. as a means of inducing Japan to assure increased U.S. exports of auto parts to Japan is not among the better ways!

The Japanese economy is suffering from a protracted recession. During the past four years, Japan's GDP has hovered between slightly positive and slightly negative growth. Corporate profits have been low or negative in most sectors of industry. Japan's banking system has amassed an enormous volume of bad debts (i.e., nonperforming loans)—estimated between 21 trillion yen (240 billion dollars) and 100 trillion yen (1.2 trillion dollars), representing a quarter of the economy's GDP, and several times larger than the S&L fiasco in the United States of the 1980s. For the first time in Japan's postwar history, new lending in Japan has, since mid-1994, been below the prior year's level, and has continued to fall.

If Japan yields to the U.S. sanctions-backed threat—to "buy my cars, or else," as *The Economist* describes it—the additional imports of cars and auto parts will add further deflationary pressure to the economy's already protracted recession. Quite probably, Japanese imports of goods and services other than cars will decrease, resulting in minimal change in the bilateral current account balances between the U.S. and Japan. So, the Japanese economy will be hurt, and the U.S. economy will not appreciably benefit.

There is a better way—one that would seek to redress Japan's chronic current account surplus (i.e., the symptom) by remedying its domestic macroeconomic imbalance (the cause), in contrast to the misguided automotive sanctions invoked by Washington.

The better way has two parts:

- a large expansion of Japan's public investment—to $300 billion, compared to the inadequate level presently planned—for repair and replacement of the enormous damage inflicted by the January Hanshin earthquake, to be financed by issuing general government revenue bonds;
- assuring that at least half this amount is open to genuinely fair, competitive bidding by foreign engineering and construction firms.

This large injection of public investment spending would provide for reconstruction of the major sections of the Hanshin Expressway that collapsed in the earthquake, as well as repair or replacement of the road and rail network, water mains, port facilities, power generating and distribution structures, telecommunications, and commercial and residential structures that were devastated by the quake. The result would be a timely stimulus to a demand-limited, deflationary economy. Because the Japanese economy has been operating at a low level (about 80 percent) of capacity, the resulting boost in demand would generate increased output without inflationary consequences. If this incremental public investment were spread over, say, three years, Japan's annual growth rate could be increased by about 2 percent above its anemic rates of the past four years, and its imports from the U.S. and the rest of the world would increase accordingly.

Furthermore, opening at least half the additional investment to genuinely fair, competitive bidding by foreign firms would result in large savings for Japanese taxpayers and bondholders. Construction costs of major U.S. firms, like Bechtel, and Fluor, and Korean ones like Hyundai, are between one-quarter and one-fifth the comparable costs of Japanese construction and engineering firms like Kajima and Mitsui. If half the repair and reconstruction projects were awarded to foreign bidders, Japan would save over $100 billion! In turn, these financial savings, by increasing the yen earnings of foreigners, would reduce Japan's current account surplus as well as the U.S. current account deficit, and would cap or reverse the excessive climb in the value of the yen in foreign exchange markets—which is a source of concern to Japanese exporters and an embarrassment to Japan's central bankers. Finally, by demonstrating flexibility and openness to cooperation with the external world, Japan would measurably enhance its global stature, as well as seize the high ground in its protracted "framework" talks with the United States.

Notwithstanding the myriad strong reasons for Japanese policy to move in this direction, the scenario will be extremely difficult to realize. To seize the opportunity presented by the tragedy of the Kobe earthquake requires a rare combination of leadership by a frail Japanese government, flexibility by the powerful Japanese economic bureaucracy, and pressure by an aroused and critical Japanese public as well as by the U.S. Unlike the application of sanctions proposed by the Clinton administration, U.S. pressure in this domain would command powerful and extensive support from the rest of the international community.

June 1995

26

China's Enlarged Economy

One of the professional secrets of people who work with supposedly "hard" data is that, in fact, the data are often "soft" and unreliable. Recently, the International Monetary Fund and the World Bank—two of the most respected sources of international economic data—provided a glimpse of this secret.

In May 1993 the Fund and the Bank announced that China's gross domestic product was between four and five times greater in 1992 than they had previously estimated it to be! (For various technical reasons, the World Bank estimates are at the higher end of this range, and the IMF's at the lower end.) According to these re-estimates, which replicate almost exactly ones made by RAND five years ago, China's economy is now the third largest in the world—after that of the United States and Japan. Together with plausible forecasts of China's economic growth in the next few decades—perhaps averaging 5 or 6 percent annually—the new Fund and Bank estimates would, within the 1990s decade, make the economy of China larger than that of Japan. Were China to sustain such a high growth rate for several decades—which is unlikely—its GDP would overtake that of the United States during the third decade of the twenty-first century.

These remarkable recalculations and projections raise two interesting questions: What accounts for the enormous discrepancy between the earlier and the current estimates by the Fund and the Bank—two of the world's supposedly most reliable and reputable data sources? And what difference, if any, will this huge change in China's current economic size and its future prospects make in the global economic and security environment during the coming decades?

The answer to the first question is straightforward. In the recent estimates of the Chinese GDP, the Fund and Bank converted the Chinese currency (yuan) figures into 1992 U.S. dollars by using a "purchasing power parity" exchange rate, whereas in their prior estimates during the past decade, they used a foreign exchange rate for the conversion. The purchasing power rate is based on the cost of a specified "market-basket" of goods and services in yuan, compared to its cost in dollars. The foreign exchange rate depends on the official rate of exchange between the yuan and the dollar quoted by the International Monetary Fund. Thus, the purchasing power exchange rate depends on the relative yuan and dollar prices of the same set of goods and services, while the foreign exchange rate depends on the relative supply of and demand for yuan and dollars in official international exchange markets. Foreign exchange rates are critically dependent on international capital movements which have little effect on PPP, while PPP is influenced by the relative prices of such nontradable services as health care, housing, and construction which have little effect on exchange rates.

Although there are some purposes for which foreign exchange rates are appropriate to use in comparing national economies, for the specific purpose of comparing the relative size of different national economies the PPP rate is clearly preferable. In published work that RAND did for the National Commission on Integrated Long-term Strategy in 1988, the PPP rate was used to make international comparisons between China's gross national product and the GNPs of more than a dozen other major national economies, including that of the United States. The estimates recently announced by the Fund and the Bank were remarkably similar to the earlier RAND results.

The IMF and World Bank are two of the most frequently cited sources of international economic data, but they are not alone in the magnitude of their mis-estimates. *Overestimates* by the OECD and by official U.S. government agencies of the national economies of East Germany and the then-Soviet Union prior to 1990 were nearly equivalent in scale to the previously cited *underestimates* of China's GDP by the Fund and the Bank. Since even these supposedly reliable data sources are sometimes prone to large errors, caution is plainly warranted in using their data. When policy choices are influenced by data derived from these and similar sources, the chosen policies may be as unreliable as the shaky data on which they are based.

The answer to the second question about what difference the reestimates of the Chinese economy make in the international arena has two parts: one economic, the other bearing on military and security matters.

A Chinese economy that is four to five times larger than it was previously believed to be, and continues to grow at a 5 to 6 percent annual rate, will play an equivalently expanded role in the world economy. In general, changes in a country's imports depend, among other factors, on the growth of its economy, as well as its size. If China's economy becomes more open to foreign imports, and if one accepts the previously cited estimates that the size of the Chinese economy is currently about 2 trillion dollars, China will become an increasingly important market for exports from the U.S. as well as from the Asia-Pacific region and the rest of the world. China is still too small to be anything approaching the "locomotive" for the rest of the world's economies that the U.S. economy was in the 1970s and the 1980s. But China, together with the rapidly growing Southeast Asian economies, amount to about 40 percent of the size of the U.S. economy, and this may be large enough to be at least a "tractor" for the rest of the world. If such other factors as successful conclusion of the Uruguay round of GATT, and adoption of growth-promoting tax policies by Asian countries, proceed in favorable and reinforcing directions, the Asia-Pacific tractor can help significantly to pull the world's economies to higher ground.

The security dimension of China's changed and changing economic size is more unsettling, as well as more uncertain. China is currently the only major country in the world whose military spending is increasing in real terms. About 8 percent of its GDP is allocated to defense to cover the current operating costs of the 4 million men and women in its armed forces, as well as the costs of military modernization. These figures compare to GDP shares of 4 percent for the United States, a little over 1 percent for Japan, and about 2 percent for the countries of Western Europe. Military allocations of this scale, from the large and growing economic base that China's GDP provides, are a source of increasing concern to China's neighbors in East Asia as well as South Asia.

Joseph Schumpeter, an economist whose interests and insights extended beyond the usual boundaries of economics, observed some four decades ago that "militarism is rooted in the autocratic state, [whereas] the bourgeois [state] is unwarlike."[1] The Asia-Pacific region, as well as the rest of the world, has much to gain from China's move from autocracy toward some semblance of bourgeois democracy—the latter, of course, "with a Chinese face."

November 1993

Note

1. Joseph Schumpeter, *Social Classes—Imperialism: Two Essays*, Meridian Books, 1955, p. 96.

27

Asia's Rise Will Advance U.S. Prosperity

Asian experts (like regional and country experts in general) come in two varieties: those whose expertise is principally based on academic credentials, and those whose expertise is principally based on experience. Although productive combinations of the two sometimes occur, each variety tends to be profoundly skeptical of the other. This mutual skepticism is amply warranted because their respective forecasts about the regions and countries in which they are expert have so often missed the boat: for example, the fall of the Berlin Wall, the collapse of the Soviet Union, the revelation of Japan's economic fault lines, the sharp decline in the strength of the "Shining Path" guerrillas in Peru, and the mullahs seizure of power in Iran. In each case the consensus forecasts of regional and country experts erred badly.

Jim Rohwer, author of *Asia Rising: Why America will Prosper as Asia's Economies Boom* (Simon & Schuster), is an expert of the second variety. He is currently director and chief economist for Asia in the Hong Kong office of CS First Boston, and previously spent four years as executive editor and Asian correspondent of the *Economist*.

Mr. Rohwer's title aptly summarizes the central thesis of a work which the author characterizes, perhaps too modestly, as "an extended piece of journalism." Indeed, it is that, but only in the best and hardly typical, sense of the term. Although the writing is light and lucid, *Asia Rising* is crammed with useful facts, as well as insightful arguments and provocative conclusions.

Mr. Rohwer foresees an Asia that will continue to be the most dynamic element in the world economy in the next generation because of its high rates of saving and investment; a large, increasingly literate and increasingly skilled labor force; an enormous and growing consumer market; and an expanding proportion of global trade. He also foresees

137

lucrative opportunities for Western business, especially American firms which are "best positioned...to compete on reasonably even terms with Japanese firms in their own backyard."

In support of this thesis, Mr. Rohwer marshals an impressive array of current data and recent research findings relating to China, India, and the countries of Northeast and Southeast Asia. His *tour d'horizon* includes the scale and patterns of Asian savings and investment, labor productivity and costs, the size of overseas Chinese investment in Asia which he characterizes as "one of the powerhouses of the world economy," and a conjectural view of "greater China"—including Taiwan, Hong Kong, and Singapore, as well as China itself—as constituting a "pole of economic growth with powers of attraction in the same league with America, Japan, and Germany."

Along the way, *Asia Rising* also provides a guide to "who's who" among Asian businessmen and companies, and a manual of do's and don'ts for foreign firms wishing to succeed in Asia. He points out, for example, that American firms are far more flexible and effective in using Asian nationals in executive positions than are Japanese firms which tend to shun locals in favor of Japanese managers.

Occasionally Mr. Rohwer's command of facts and data errs. For example, it isn't true that Foreign Direct Investment (FDI) in Asia (or elsewhere) goes "directly to build factories or buy buildings, not to buy stocks or bonds." As FDI is usually measured, purchases of equities that exceed 10 percent of a firm's total equity are included in FDI, whether or not the purchases directly add to tangible capital.

Also, even if much or most of Asia's remarkable growth in the past decade has been due to huge increases in inputs rather than in the efficiency of their use, it doesn't follow that *future* efficiency gains—that is, increases in total factor productivity—are precluded. Indeed, exactly the reverse of this argument can be made.

Another small error: if Singapore has 5,000 millionaires, as Mr. Rohwer suggests, they comprise only 0.17 percent of the city-state's 3 million people, not 0.3 percent, as he states.

But these are minor points that are not central to the buoyant optimism of the book's message. Three other points are more central to the argument, as well as controversial.

In accounting for Asia's past record and its bright future prospects, Mr. Rohwer accords primacy to two attributes. One of these is what he terms "enlightened authoritarianism." Its advantage, he suggests, is that it can push economic progress effectively because it accords "less heed to special interests" than does "lobby-based democracy." In support of this proposition, Mr. Rohwer frequently and favorably quotes the views of Singapore's "soft" authoritarian, Lee Kwan Yew, who contrasts the strong economic performance of authoritarian China with the laggard record of India—the latter being a "lobby-based democracy."

The argument is unconvincing because the adjectives it employs, in effect, make it tautological. To be sure, authoritarianism that pursues "enlightened" policies—that is, sensible fiscal, monetary, and social policies—will more effectively promote development than "lobby-based democracy" which does not. But, it is worth recalling that the history of many countries—for example, in Latin America—has been replete with cases of authoritarian leaders who were "unenlightened" and who paid excessive "heed to special interests." And, on the other side of the coin, some countries—for example, Israel, Taiwan, and Costa Rica—have managed to combine democracy with "enlightened" policies, thereby promoting effective economic development. Authoritarianism is often "*un*enlightened" and democracy can be "enlightened."

The second central point in Mr. Rohwer's argument will be objected to vociferously by some readers. He contends that one of Asia's major advantages over much of the rest of the world lies in the smaller, more limited, and more focused role it assigns to governments and to public policy. He writes:

> The nub of the Asian idea of public policy is that governments should not do much to temper the hazards of life, particularly the often harsh consequences of fast technological and economic change. Asia's governments have tended to offer little social protection, such as pay-as-you-go pensions, unemployment insurance, or state-provided health care. Government spending in Asia accounts for an unusually small share of economic activity; and, in comparison with Western countries, very little of Asian government spending goes for transfer payments from the pockets of one class of taxpayers into those of another class. Except in such places as India and the Philippines, even less of Asian governments' money goes for current spending on such things as civil servants' salaries. Conversely, Asian governments devote proportionally more of their more modest spending to investment, especially in education.

> Still, although Asia's governments have been pro-business as well as small—meaning they leave much economic (and even social) decisionmaking to the competitive interplay in marketplaces—these governments have in general been as reluctant to safeguard individual companies as they have been to protect individual people.

Mr. Rohwer contends that Asia has done well because it has been characterized by "small government and strong society" and, further, that its society has been strong *because* government has been relatively small.

In the penultimate chapter of *Asia Rising,* Mr. Rohwer addresses "War and Peace." He acknowledges that "in the first half of the 1990s, Asia has had the fastest growth in arsenals and the arms trade," and he accepts the fact that China's actual military spending is well above its reported spending. But, he concludes, "this military buildup is far from being as menacing as it sounds," and so his optimism about Asia's ability to maintain peace and avoid war remains unaffected by these signals.

It is to be hoped that he is right. On the other hand, with 11,000 miles of what its leaders view as exposed and vulnerable borders, China may feel justified in aggressively pursuing modernization and enhancement of its military capabilities. The danger is that what China may view as amply warranted by *defensive* considerations may be seen by its neighbors—in India, Southeast Asia, and Taiwan—as threatening. This tension, may, in the course of events, lead to conflict.

His conclusion—that the role of U.S. military presence in Asia is vital to preserve stability in the region—is one that this reviewer endorses, although with less confidence than Mr. Rohwer expresses that this presence will be maintained into the twenty-first century.

December 1995

28

The United States and Japan:
"Revisionism" Revisited

The trouble with the Japan "revisionists," whose intellectual guru is Chalmers Johnson, is their affliction with "cognitive dissonance": a psychological aberration in which a belief is held with such utter conviction that events and data incompatible with it are denied or reinterpreted with as much creative unrealism as necessary to preserve the original belief. Mr. Johnson enthusiastically expounds the revisionist ideology in *"Japan: Who Governs?—The Rise of the Developmental State"* (W.W. Norton). Predictably, he ignores the quotidian occurrences in Japan and the outside world that contradict it.

The revisionist ideology consists of fourteen essays, some previously published and others appearing for the first time.

The lead proposition is that Japan's form of capitalism differs fundamentally from that of the United States. Japan is a vigorous and ascending "capitalist developmental state," while the U.S. is a tired and declining "capitalist regulatory state." Answering the question posed in the book's title, Mr. Johnson asserts that Japan is governed by "soft authoritarianism," a "planned economy" in which the dominant role of the State is exercised by a "covert elite," consisting at its pinnacle of the "economic bureaucracy" (specifically, the best and the brightest graduates of Tokyo University in the Ministries of Finance and International Trade and Industry), the Liberal Democratic Party, and the leaders of big business.

The second proposition is that Japan's ruling elite devises and implements "mercantilist industrial and trade policies," makes "capital available on a preferred basis to strategic industries," and provides "incentives that impose long-term perspectives on company operations."

Finally, Mr. Johnson asserts that Japan's centrally guided economy foreshadows its continued ascendance in the world economy, while the United States, unless it can "copy or match" the Japanese model, is consigned to continued decline and "lost economic influence."

Mr. Johnson's revisionist creed has many relevant and insightful things to say about the Japanese system. That system *is* different, and unquestionably has realized many extraordinary accomplishments. The weakness of revisionism is its unbalanced assessment of the difference and the accomplishments. Ironically, Mr. Johnson, who repeatedly and sometimes venomously criticizes American policymakers in general and "English-speaking economists" in particular, for their "ideological blinders," is the victim of his own ideological blinders. This is the "cognitive dissonance" syndrome!

Abundant evidence that contradicts the revisionist tableau is ignored or suppressed in his revisionist view. To cite a few among innumerable examples, Japan's GDP is now entering its fifth consecutive year of stagnation, industrial production at the end of 1994 was 5.5 percent below that of 1990 (the corresponding figure for the U.S. is 15 percent higher than in 1990!), Japan's rate of measured technological progress over the past eight years has been close to zero (compared to an annual average of about 1 percent in the U.S.), and average labor productivity in Japan is 17 percent below that in the U.S. Nor does Japan's response to the Kobe earthquake give much credence to the revisionist view of the governing "covert elite's" wisdom and efficiency.

A strikingly different picture of the U.S.-Japan comparison is painted by Nicholas Spulber's *The American Economy: The Struggle for Supremacy in the 21st Century* (Cambridge University Press). Mr. Spulber, a professor of economics at Indiana University, analyzes the reasons for expecting continued superior performance of the U.S. economy compared to that of Japan in the twenty-first century. His book, a survey of the U.S. economy from 1947 to the present, reads like an edited transcript of an economics survey course, in this respect comparing unfavorably with Mr. Johnson's more eloquent prose. Nevertheless, Mr. Spulber's book lucidly presents data and analysis of U.S. economic growth over the past four decades, the changing nature of government-business relations, the strength of U.S. technological progress, and the "proliferation of strategic international alliances, joint venture mergers, and acquisitions of foreign firms" in which the United States plays the leading role.

With this as background, Mr. Spulber turns to the challenges posed by both Japan and Germany in the twenty-first century. In considering the role of government policy, he draws the usual contrast between the macroeconomic (fiscal and monetary) policy focus of the United States, and the more intrusive microeconomic industrial policy of MITI in "picking winners" among putative strategic industries. Unlike Mr. Johnson, he views MITI's record as both mixed and exaggerated. Whether Japan's economic achievements have been due to, or in spite of, MITI and industrial policy is an open question, for Mr. Spulber. Actually, this view is held by an increasing number of analysts inside, as well as outside, Japan—a revision of revisionism is already under way!

Mr. Spulber's view of the U.S. economic outlook relative to that of Japan and Germany is so far from that of Mr. Johnson that one might infer they are observing different countries, if not different planets. In Mr. Spulber's view, the U.S. economy in the twenty-first century "will continue to move forward energetically and enterprisingly if growth and change are left to the private economy...[without] centrally devised and highly-subsidized industrial policies and export strategies."

March 1995

29

Rivalry and Disputes Among the Big Three

In *A Cold Peace: America, Japan, Germany, and the Struggle for Supremacy* (Times Books/Random House), Jeffrey E. Garten argues that disputes and rivalries among the Big Three will dominate international affairs in the next decade and beyond. These confrontations, he writes, will arise over such issues as trade policy and protectionism, foreign investment and industrial policy, immigration and refugees, global alliances and burden sharing.

There is both sense and nonsense in Mr. Garten's views. He is on solid ground in saying that "the international setting (will) be radically different from what we have known," and that the United States can expect to have serious disputes with both Japan and Germany. Among the corroborating indicators are the recent and continuing differences in their respective positions in GATT, on assistance to the republics of the Commonwealth of Independent States, on peacemaking in the Balkans, on coordination of their national monetary and fiscal policies, and on international environmental policies.

Garten also has sensible and original things to say about the reasons "why domestic policy and international policy must be meshed together...[because] the foreign policy agenda is so dominated by issues rooted in policies at home—trade, investment, currencies, technological cooperation"; about the different characteristics of capitalism in the three countries (he labels the American system a "liberal market economy," that of Japan, a "developmental economy," and that of Germany, a "social market economy"); and about the differing "degree of openness" in each of the three societies.

However, Garten's frequent display of good sense and insight is accompanied by equally impressive lapses from them. The lapses are conceptual, empirical, and judgmental.

One conceptual flaw inheres in a framework that, by its preoccupation with the *soi-disant* Big Three, accords remarkably little attention to such other major current and prospective players as China, Russia, India, Brazil, Korea, and other regional powers. Notwithstanding the economic and financial scope of the Three, the influence of these "n-th" countries is likely to loom much larger in the new and impending disorderly world than Garten acknowledges.

Another conceptual flaw is Garten's implicit presumption of monolithicity in what "Washington," "Tokyo," or "Berlin" does, and represents, or how each will behave, or progress in the future. The reality is more complex and diverse. In each of the Three, significant entities and individuals—corporations, professional associations, scientists, financial institutions—may act differently from the simplistic uniformities that Garten attributes to them.

Furthermore, the Big Three also have major common interests; for example, convertible currencies, protection of their sea and air lines of communication, progress toward peace in the Middle East, and toward marketization and democratization in the republics of the former Soviet Union. Such common interests provide a much broader base for cooperation and collaboration among the United States, Japan, and Germany than is envisaged in *A Cold Peace*.

Some of the empirical data scattered throughout the book are erroneous or apocryphal. The United States certainly doesn't "sell or produce" 20 percent of its GNP abroad, as Garten asserts. U.S. exports of goods and services are 8 percent of its GNP, and the only part of foreign production by U.S. subsidiaries that is included in the calculation of GNP is factor income from abroad (about 2 percent of GNP), not their total production.

Another empirical lapse is reflected by Garten's statement that, with respect to shouldering "greater global responsibilities...Tokyo and Berlin are unlikely to move one inch more than they have to." Japan's financial undertakings in the environmental area at the Rio Summit in June 1992, and Germany's enormous resource transfers to Russia and the other republics are counter examples.

The judgmental flaws in *A Cold Peace* frequently occur because the author is captivated by the many writings of recent years that bemoan the problems and shortcomings of the U.S. economy, and that forecast the decline of American power and influence in the world. To be sure, these problems warrant serious attention and careful analysis, as well as sensible remedial actions. But remedying the serious U.S. problems in education, drugs, crime, health costs, and productivity growth isn't helped by an unrelenting disposition to magnify them, while ignoring equally serious, although different, domestic problems in Germany and Japan.

Garten pays little attention to the problems that Japan faces in the aging of its population, the shaken confidence produced by the 60 percent drop in the Nikkei Index, MITI's efforts to enhance "the quality of Japanese life" through a shorter work week and through higher levels of per capita consumption and recreation, probably leading to a more slowly growing economy, although perhaps a happier society.

It is also likely that both the costs and time required for successful German unification have been drastically underestimated, resulting in increased inflationary pressures, a redirection of Germany's exports toward the Eastern *länder*, a fundamental change in Germany's ability to export capital abroad, and serious stresses and strains in Germany's social structure.

It is no more sensible to underestimate the problems confronting one's competitors than to be complacent about one's own.

August 1992

Part IV

Transforming the Russian and Ukrainian Economies

30

Transforming Command Economies into Market Economies: Problems, Solutions, Obstacles

Over the past century, economists and other intellectuals have produced an enormous literature on how to convert capitalist market economies into centrally planned, socialist ones. The notable contributors include the Webbs (Sidney and Beatrice), Oskar Lange, Abba Lerner, Joan Robinson, Nicholas Kaldor, Paul Sweezy, Wassily Leontief, J. K. Galbraith, and innumerable others.

It is ironic that the reverse problem of converting socialist economies into capitalist ones has received scant attention. The writings of Friedrich Hayek, Joseph Schumpeter, Milton Friedman, and P. T. Bauer are partial exceptions, but their focus has usually been elsewhere: namely, exposing the errors made by the advocates of socialism, rather than charting the transformation to market economies. Hence, there is no general theory to draw on in addressing the crucial economic policy problem of the 1990s: how to transform command economies into market economies.

Recognition of the failures of command economies, and the need to transform them, is the reason why the rhetoric of "markets" and "marketizing" is definitely "in" in the 1990s. But the unanimity and ubiquity with which markets are advocated—in the Soviet Union and its principal republics, as well as in the countries of Eastern Europe, China, and the third world—obscure the profound divergences about what the terms mean, and what they imply for transforming command economies into market-oriented ones. These divergences are latent in such frequently used oxymorons as "market socialism" (a term invented by the Hungarian economist, Janos Kornai, but subsequently rejected by him), or "regulated socialist markets" (a term favored periodically by Gorbachev and certain "conservative" Soviet economists), or what some Chinese leaders envisage as a system between capitalism and socialism which they describe as "socialism with Chinese characteristics."

The underlying disagreements concern the details about transforming command systems into market systems. In this case, as in others, the details are crucial. They relate to whether markets should be "free" or "regulated," competitive or "social"; whether the market's intended reach should be extensive and predominant, or partial and limited; whether transformation should be rapid or gradual; whether the emergent system should be open to international competition and should allow free movement of capital and commodities, or be protected from them; and, finally, whether the scope of the government sector, at the end of the process, should be extensive, or narrowly circumscribed.

That these divergences are so deep is not surprising. The rhetoric of markets and marketizing has been adopted by a remarkably diverse group of advocates, including Communists, ex-Communists, erstwhile central planners, Social Democrats, "liberals," and "radicals," as well as new and aspiring entrepreneurs in the transforming command economies. The advocates also include an ideologically mixed set of experts, advisers, consultants, and commentators in the West, including some—like Jacques Delors, Secretary General of the European Community, and Jacques Attali, Head of the new Bank for European Reconstruction and Development—who have until recently favored transformation of capitalist economies into socialist ones.

As a result of this diversity of views and viewers, the ensuing policy debate has often been muddled, the essentials of the transformation process frequently misunderstood, and its costs generally exaggerated. Indeed, transforming command (or "non-market") economies into market ones, although a challenging problem, is more tractable, and the costs and "pain" of the transition should be considerably less, than much of the debate has implied—provided the transformation is pursued comprehensively and aggressively.

Transformation as a Systems Problem

The generic problems of transforming a command economy into a market economy are essentially the same whether the locale is the Soviet Union, Eastern Europe, China, or many of the centrally controlled economies of the Third World. To be sure, there are differences in historical circumstances, cultural affinities, institutional antecedents, and the existing physical, social, and political infrastructures. But the differences are incidental to an essentially similar task. Transformation depends on implementing simultaneously, or at least contemporaneously, a package of six closely linked and mutually supporting elements:

- Monetary reform to ensure control of the money supply and credit;
- Fiscal control to assure budgetary balance and to limit monetization of a budget deficit if one occurs;
- Price and wage deregulation, to link prices and wages to costs and productivity, respectively;
- Privatization, legal protection of property rights, and the breakup of state monopolies, to provide for competition, as well as worker and management incentives that reflect changes in relative market prices;
- A social "safety net" to protect those who may become unemployed as transformation proceeds; and
- Currency convertibility to link the transforming economy to the world economy and to competition in international markets.

These six elements are mutually supporting and interactive. The first two—monetary reform and fiscal control—and the fifth—the social safety net—create the broad macroeconomic environment that enables the incentive mechanisms of the other three elements to move resources toward more efficient and growth-promoting uses. The government's role is both crucial and paradoxical: crucial in initiating all of the elements, yet paradoxical because the process that the government initiates is intended to diminish its ensuing role, displacing its overextended functions and reducing its size in favor of market mechanisms.

Each of the six elements is less likely to be effective without the reciprocal support provided by the other elements. Hence, attempts to reform non-market economies by piecemeal steps are more likely to founder than to succeed.

Consider, for example, the link between the first two elements. Monetary reform is necessary to limit growth of the money supply to a rate that accords with the growth of real output. It is also a necessary means to provide access to credit on the basis of borrowers' economic capabilities and their associated risks, rather than on the basis of their political connections or credentials. A competent entrepreneur with a good idea should be able to obtain credit that is not available to someone whose principal distinction is membership in the governing political party or kinship to a government official.

Fiscal reform requires a budget process that constrains government expenditures to a level approximating that of revenues, and precludes or limits "off-budget" subsidies and other transactions that would disrupt monetary discipline, as well as budgetary balance. Recourse to extra-budgetary subsidies to bail out deficit-ridden state enterprises has been a standard procedure in the Soviet Union, China, and other command economies. Fiscal and monetary reform should preclude its recurrence. Usually, the complementarity between monetary reform and fiscal reform is facilitated by institutional separation between the Finance Ministry (or Treasury), and the Central Bank or banking system.

In turn, the third element—deregulation of prices and wages—requires monetary and fiscal restraint if deregulation is to change relative prices by linking them, as well as wages, to real costs and productivity, while avoiding general inflation. Goods that are in short supply or are costly to produce should experience price increases relative to those that are more abundant and less costly. In turn, these price increases provide signals and incentives for increased and more efficient production. Similarly, wages paid for more productive labor and skills should be expected to rise relative to those that are less productive. Moreover, the newly established parities among costs and prices should operate in the public sector, as well as the private sector.

For deregulation of prices and wages to promote efficient use of resources requires contemporaneous implementation of the fourth element: privatization, legal protection of property rights, and the breakup of state monopolies into competing entities. This requires an appropriate legal code and appropriate procedures for resolving disputes over property transactions and acquisitions. It also requires a choice among several alternative ways of changing from state ownership to private ownership—an issue on which there is considerable controversy among policymakers, economists, lawyers, and financiers.

For example, equity shares in state enterprises can be issued to enterprise workers and management, while reserving some proportion of the shares for local government and foreign investors, as well as providing for resale of the shares with or without a specified holding period. This method, favored by Paul Roberts among others, has the advantage of simplicity and clarity; its putative disadvantage is the ostensible unfairness of a process in which some of the new shareholders would be losers, while others would realize gains, due in both cases to the arbitrary circumstance of where they had been previously employed.

Another mode of privatization is to issue enterprise shares to the general public on a random basis, rather than determining enterprise ownership on the basis of employment. In this case, everyone has an equal chance of picking a winner or loser among the hundreds or thousands of state enterprises that typically exist in the command economies. Windfall gains that result from a random process are, it can be argued, more equitable than those that result from the accident of prior employment.

Perhaps the simplest method of privatization is to auction enterprises to their highest bidders—limiting or excluding participation by non-nationals. This method, favored by Czechoslovakian economist (and Finance Minister) Vaclav Klaus, as well as others, has sometimes been criticized on the grounds that those most likely to have ample funds enabling them to win the bidding are the black marketeers and former Communist Party nomenklatura.

Still another method is to issue vouchers to the public representing potential claims on the shares of enterprises to be privatized, and then to invite foreign bankers or mutual fund managers to bid for the public vouchers, on the basis of the portfolio selection criteria favored by the competing funds. The public would surrender their vouchers in return for shares in the mutual funds that appealed to individual voucher holders. Variants of this method of privatization have been advanced by Jeff Sachs and several Polish economists.

All of these methods would result in the creation of a resale market for equities and mutual fund shares. Contrary to some of the debate on this issue, none of the methods requires that state enterprises be carefully evaluated *before* privatization is accomplished. Choosing among the alternative methods requires assessment of their respective advantages (for example, simplicity, comprehensibility, and speed), as well as their disadvantages (for example, distributional unfairness and inequity).

In any event, whichever method or methods of privatization are selected—and experimentation with several is advisable because none is clearly preferable to the others—their success remains linked to the other elements of the transformation package. Unless rewards are linked to asset ownership, and unless such rewards can be accumulated legally, incentives to innovate and to increase productivity will be impaired. Effective supply responses to price and wage deregulation depend on the incentives provided by private ownership and accumulation. Moreover, private ownership is essential for market forces to provide an effective "stick," as well as "carrot." If ownership is in the hands of the state, the discipline imposed by market competition will be attenuated, if not eliminated. When state enterprises are confronted by losses, they typically evade or ignore the threat of bankruptcy that private enterprises would face if confronted by similar losses.

It has sometimes been argued—by Gorbachev in the Soviet Union and Li Peng in China, as well as by others both inside and outside the reforming command economies—that privatization is neither necessary nor would it be effective. The contention accompanying this argument is that privatization leads to wide gaps between rich and poor, and that a "culture of envy" has become strongly pervasive and ingrained, especially in the Soviet Union. Consequently, it is argued, privatization won't be tolerated, and won't be effective if it is imposed.

To the extent these attitudes exist, they may be attributable to long-standing and widespread experience that sharp disparities in income distribution, and in levels of living, have been associated with political preferment or corruption, rather than with private ownership, innovation, and productivity. Resentment against the sharp disparities prevailing in command Communist systems has been due to the widespread conviction that the rich and powerful have acquired their positions through political clout or favoritism, rather than economic innovation or productivity. Such resentment is not unknown in market economies. Nevertheless, in moving from command to market economies, private ownership plays a crucial role by providing the incentive structure required for markets to function efficiently. To avoid socially unacceptable disparities in income distribution is a responsibility of public expenditure and tax policies, within the context of private ownership and market competition.

The fifth element—establishment of a social security system as a "safety net"—is also essential for the transformation process to succeed. Without it, the process as a whole may create a fear of widespread unemployment (although I will suggest later why increased unemployment, when accurately measured, may be considerably less than what has been feared), as well as social stress, political instability, and a serious impediment to the transition to a market system.

In most command economies, social protection—against illness, disability, age, and unemployment—has principally been the responsibility of state enterprises. As privatization proceeds, these responsibilities are likely to become one of the principal functions of government, financed by taxation as well as by payments levied on the insured. In the initial stage of transformation, taxation will probably have to bear most of the burden although, for reasons to be discussed later, the real *incremental* burden imposed on the economy by the social safety net is likely to be less than is usually assumed.

The final element—currency convertibility—is essential to complete the transformation process by linking internal markets and their prices, wages, productivities, and technologies, to those of international markets. This linkage provides the opportunity for comparative costs and comparative advantage to operate for the benefit of the transforming national economy. By having a convertible currency, the transforming economy can determine those goods and services it can produce at relatively low cost compared to the costs of other countries, and those it produces at relatively high cost. In response to convertibility, exports of the relatively low-cost goods will expand, as will imports of the relatively high-cost ones.

If the other elements of the package—especially monetary and fiscal discipline, and market-determined prices—are effectively implemented, currency convertibility with a floating exchange rate can be embarked upon and sustained with minimal hard currency reserves, contrary to a frequent argument about the need for large reserves as a precondition for convertibility. Poland's establishment of a convertible zloty at the beginning of 1990 was accomplished notwithstanding the country's net foreign exchange indebtedness of over $50 billion! Although Poland received a foreign exchange stabilization loan of $1 billion from the United States, none of it was drawn upon in the ensuing year. Instead, with its convertible currency system, Poland accumulated hard currency foreign exchange holdings of over $2 billion in the ensuing year.

The interactions and mutually supporting relationships among the six elements of the transformation process are summarized in Fig. 30.1 below. The solid lines indicate the contribution by one element to the effectiveness of another element to which the arrowhead points. (For example, monetary and fiscal reform contribute reciprocally to supporting one another, while both of them contribute to the effectiveness of price and wage deregulation.)

FIGURE 30.1
Components of Transformation of Command Economies

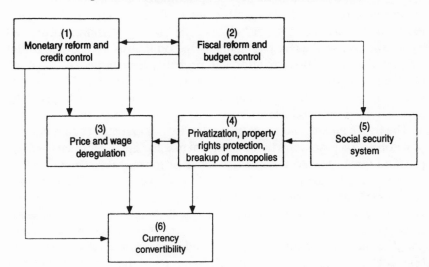

In sum, the process of transforming command, non-market economies to market economies is both better understood and more tractable than might be inferred from much of the public debate. Transformation is a systems process encompassing all of the interactive and mutually supporting elements described above. The debate which disputes this systems view argues instead that one or another of the six elements is not essential, or is of higher priority than other elements, or should precede the others.

For example, as noted earlier, Gorbachev in the Soviet Union, Li Peng in China, and some of their "conservative" advisers, contend that private ownership of productive assets, including land, is inessential, while its incentive effects can be obtained through leases administered by the State. In opposition to this view is the position of American banker Leif Olsen, Soviet economist Nikolai Shmelev and others, who assert that private ownership in general, and privatization of State enterprises in particular, are the most fundamental ingredients of economic restructuring. Along the same line, Canadian economist Reuven Brenner argues that reform of the legal system, to assure and protect property rights, is the essential precondition for any further reform efforts.

Another stance, associated with economists Gregory Grossman, Igor Birman, and Judy Shelton, emphasizes the primacy of monetary and fiscal reform and, in the Soviet case, substantial reduction of the existing monetary stock—the so-called "ruble overhang"—as an indispensable precondition for preventing the rampant inflation that would otherwise follow price deregulation and other reform measures.

Indeed, I have previously advanced some of these views myself. In earlier writings on the Soviet Union, I suggested that price and wage deregulation, combined with the mandatory conversion of large ruble holdings into long-term, non-tradable bonds, were necessary and sufficient measures for moving the Soviet economy toward marketization. And in subsequent work in China, I focused on the central importance of currency convertibility in achieving marketization. Now, it seems clear to me, for both theoretical and practical reasons, that trying to transform a command system into a market system without the synergy provided by all of these elements is like trying to swim with one arm and leg rather than two of each. To attempt the transformation process on a piecemeal and gradual basis would be—to use another simile—like trying to shift a country's driving practices from the left side of the road to the right side in stages. The risk of serious accident is manifestly greater than if the change is accomplished all at once.

Some Recent Experience

Among the command economies that have attempted to transform themselves into market economies, Poland's efforts have been the most far-reaching. Yet these changes—although more extensive and effective than restructuring efforts elsewhere—have been incomplete. On the positive side, Poland's budget deficit has been reduced from approximately 8 percent to about 1 percent of GNP. Monetary discipline has been encouraged by separating the central bank from the treasury. Ninety percent of all prices have been decontrolled, and convertibility of the zloty has been maintained at a stable rate since January 1990, with exports increasing, hard currency imports declining, and a resulting trade surplus of over $2 billion.

These are significant accomplishments, although not sufficient. To date, the Poles have only partially privatized. They have deferred the breaking up of state monopolies and delayed the wage reform necessary to create proper incentives for labor and management. Hence, supply responses and sectoral resource reallocations have been inhibited, and output, employment, and inflation have suffered. Still, if one were grading the various country efforts, Poland would receive a strong B.

By contrast, Gorbachev's faltering attempts to move toward a market economy, and to combine the defunct Ryzhkov and Shatalin plans would barely rate a D. Thus far, controls remain on the prices of essential consumer goods, as well as basic commodities like oil, gas, lumber, steel, and other key goods and services, such as transportation and communications. Although their "established" or official prices have been raised, the levels and parities among them are determined by central planners, not by the market. Budgetary spending is supposed to be curtailed, yet subsidies for many enterprises have been maintained. State enterprises are supposed to resort to "self-financing" to an increasing extent to meet their financial needs. In fact, credit extensions evidently are available to them if stringencies arise, especially if the enterprises can argue that financing is needed to fulfill state contracts. Although state enterprises are intended to be privatized, no timetable or operational plan for doing so has been established. And to the extent that convertibility of the ruble is mentioned at all, the intention is that it will be "gradual," without any indication of when or how this will be accomplished. And even these limited measures have been set back as a result of the recent increased reliance on KGB and military authority in running the economy.

China's economic restructuring efforts probably rank somewhere between Poland and the Soviet Union—perhaps warranting a grade of C, probably higher for its rural reform in the early 1980s, but lower than C for its meager reform efforts in the urban sector before and after the Tiananmen tragedy of June 1989. While there has been extensive price deregulation, wages remain largely fixed. Limited progress has been made in the direction of privatization, especially through joint ventures with foreign investors. State enterprises remain largely responsible for social security, thereby burdening them with high cost obligations and impeding any prospective progress toward the breaking up and privatization of these enterprises. Although there has been no explicit move toward convertibility, the establishment of fairly effective monetary and fiscal discipline has helped to create a situation in which the black market value of the ren min bi is only about 30 percent below the official rate.

Transitional Costs of Transformation

It is widely assumed in much of the ongoing debate that the transitional costs of transforming command economies into market ones will be extremely high, as well as protracted. But this assessment is flawed by a fundamental measurement error. In fact, the costs and pain of the transition are likely to be less than is usually presumed, if the process is pursued along the inclusive and expeditious lines described earlier.

The critical error arises from comparing real levels of output, employment, and prices in the post-transformation market environment with the spurious recorded levels of the prior command environment. For example, it has been said that Poland's GNP has declined by 16 percent, unemployment has risen to more than one million, and inflation has increased by 35 percent more than wages since Poland's "crash" economic reform program was initiated in January 1990. Similar or greater disruptions have been forecast by Gorbachev and others in the Soviet Union if "radical" restructuring were to proceed there. All of these figures are wide of the mark.

In non-market systems, like that of the Soviet Union, or China, or Poland prior to 1990, recorded output is typically and substantially overestimated due to several factors: (1) underestimation of "hidden" inflation that takes the form of maintaining constant prices for products of decreasing quality, or establishing higher prices for products that are reclassified to reflect apparent, but not actual, increases in quality. (In the Soviet Union, it has recently been estimated that the annual rate of inflation in recent years has probably been two or three times the previously accepted rate of about two percent); (2) inclusion of physical, but valueless, output—for example, shoes that consumers won't buy, bulldozers that are too hazardous to use and too costly to fix; (3) fraudulent reporting—the padding of reported data *(pripiski)* to meet or exceed established production norms; and (4) data manipulation for internal or external propaganda purposes.

Such factors probably account for overestimates of at least 25 percent of recorded GNP in the Soviet Union and other non-market systems. It is significant that estimates of the size of the Soviet GNP relative to that of the United States by CIA (as well as by the State Committee on Statistics in the Soviet Union) have placed the figure at about 50 percent, whereas estimates by other economists—Soviet as well as American and European—have placed the figure between 14 percent and about 30 percent! The 14 percent estimate is by academician Vladimir Tikhonov, and Victor Belkin. Soviet economists Vasili Selyunin and Grigorii Khanin have placed the figure at about 20 to 25 percent, and Anders Aslund and Igor Birman have estimated it at about 30 percent.[1] It is also significant that East Germany's per capita GNP in 1987 was estimated by both the CIA and the World Bank at about 88 percent of West Germany's, while more accurate estimates since unification suggest a figure of less than 50 percent!

Similarly, comparisons between post-transformation and pre-transformation unemployment are misleading because they are based on unemployment that is visible in the market economy, but do not allow for the make-work, featherbedding, and pay-without-product unemployment that is hidden in the pre-transformation, non-market system. The employment realities are suggested by the familiar Soviet joke: "We pretend to work, and they pretend to pay us."

Finally, it is misleading to compare post-transformation "inflation" with pre-transformation's apparent price stability. Transformation to a market system converts inflation that has typically been "hidden" in the non-market system—but reflected in long and uncertain queues, as well as declining product quality—into visible price increases in the market system.

When properly measured, the economic costs of the transition—in the accurate sense of opportunity costs—should be much less than suggested by most comments and estimates.

Why is Transformation Faltering?

If transformation to a market system is more tractable and the attendant costs are likely to be lower than is commonly assumed, why has progress been lacking (as in the Soviet Union), or very limited (as in China), or at best only modest (as in Poland)?

The question relates rather more to the politics than to the economics of transformation, more to the motivation and capacity of potential leadership and organizations than to understanding the policies necessary for moving forward. Part of the answer lies in the fact that there are deep underlying divergences among many of those who intone free market rhetoric and slogans, but are themselves decidedly ambivalent about the desirability of real system transformation. Hence, they seek reasons or excuses for delaying and temporizing, even while solemnly acknowledging the necessity for eventual systemic change. To profess a belief in free markets, together with an intention of maintaining the political dominance of the Communist Party, as does the leadership of both the Soviet Union and China, is an oxymoron.

Transforming command economies into market economies inevitably means winners and losers, although in the aggregate, the economy will gain more than it loses. In the Soviet Union, the issue is further complicated by the likelihood that the economy that gains will be that of the republics, while the loser will be that of the union. The practical problem created by impending transformation is that the reigning leadership in the ostensibly transforming economies—the Soviet Union, China, Romania, Bulgaria—are very likely to be among the losers in terms of their power, privilege, and prestige, as well as those of their principal associates. Hence, while they may use the rhetoric of markets and competition, their interests induce, if not compel, them to temporize, to delay, and perhaps to incapacitate the transformation process.

Spring 1991

Note

1. See my testimony before the Senate Foreign Relations Committee, "Estimating the Size and Growth of the Soviet Economy," July 16, 1990. See also, Henry S. Rowen and Charles Wolf, Jr., (eds.), *The Impoverished Superpower: Perestroika and the Soviet Military Burden*, ICS Press, San Francisco, 1990, especially Chapter 1 by Anders Aslund, "How Small is Soviet National Income?"

31

The Ingredients of Transforming Command Economies

It is widely believed that the transitional costs of transforming the command economies of Eastern Europe, the Soviet Union, and China into market economies will be extremely high, as well as protracted. But this assessment is flawed by a fundamental measurement error. In fact, the costs and pain of the transition are likely to be considerably less than is usually presumed, provided the transformation is pursued comprehensively and aggressively.

The error arises from comparing real levels of output, employment, and prices in the posttransformation market environment with the spurious recorded levels of the prior command environment. For example, it is said that Poland's GNP has declined by 16 percent, unemployment has risen to 1 million, and inflation has risen by 35 percent more than wages since Poland's "crash" economic program was initiated in January 1990. Similar or greater disruptions have been forecast by Gorbachev and Ryzhkov if "radical" restructuring were to proceed in the Soviet Union.

All of these figures are wide of the mark.

In nonmarket systems, like that of the Soviet Union or of Poland prior to 1990, recorded output is typically overestimated due to several factors: failure to allow for deterioration in product quality that predictably occurs when enterprise performance depends on meeting quantitative norms rather than producing net market value, inclusion of physical, but valueless, output (for example, shoes that consumers won't buy, bulldozers that are too hazardous to use and too costly to fix), fraudulent reporting—the padding of reported data (*pripiski*)—to meet or exceed norms, data manipulation for propaganda purposes, and so on.

Such factors probably account for overestimates of at least 25 percent in recorded GNP in the Soviet Union and other nonmarket systems. Significantly, East Germany's per capita GNP in 1987 was estimated by CIA and the World Bank at 88 percent of West Germany's, while more accurate recent estimates suggest a figure of less than 50 percent!

Similarly, comparisons between posttransformation and pretransformation unemployment are misleading because they are based on unemployment that is visible in the market economy, but do not allow for the make-work, featherbedding, and pay-without-product unemployment that is hidden in the pretransformation, nonmarket system. The realities are suggested by the familiar Soviet joke: "we pretend to work, and they pretend to pay us!"

Finally, it is misleading to compare posttransformation "inflation" with pretransformation's apparent price stability. Transformation to a market system converts inflation that has typically been "hidden" in the nonmarket system—but reflected in long and uncertain queues, as well as declining product quality—into visible price increases in the market regime.

In sum, the usual estimates of the economic costs of transforming nonmarket to market systems are distorted because they compare exaggerated estimates of pretransformation economic performance with more accurate estimates of posttransformation performance. The real economic value of Poland's current GNP probably equals or exceeds that of the prior nonmarket, command system.

Although the usual estimates exaggerate the transitional costs associated with transformation to a market system, the challenge of effectively transforming command economies to market economies remains formidable—formidable but tractable. Its tractability depends on implementing jointly a package of six mutually supporting elements: monetary reform, to ensure control of credit and the money supply; fiscal control, to assure budgetary balance and to limit monetization of a budget deficit if one arises; price and wage deregulation, to link prices and wages to costs and productivity; privatization, legal protection of property rights, and breakup of state monopolies, to provide entrepreneurial and labor incentives that reflect changing market prices; a social "safety net," to protect those who may become unemployed as transformation proceeds; and currency convertibility, to link the transforming economy to the world economy and to competition in international markets.

These elements are mutually supporting and interactive: the first two create the macroeconomic environment that enables the incentive mechanisms of the other elements to move resources toward more efficient uses.

Each of the six elements is less likely to be effective without the reciprocal support provided by the other elements.

For example, if prices are deregulated without simultaneously establishing control of the money supply and imposing fiscal restraint, inflation and inconvertibility will result. If, as in Poland, both monetary and budgetary control are established, prices freed, and convertibility introduced but privatization and the breakup of state monopolies are deferred, the transformation's effectiveness will be impaired. And without the necessary social safety net, the other measures may create a fear of widespread unemployment, social stress, and political instability.

Trying to transform a nonmarket to a market system without the synergy provided by all six elements is like trying to swim with one arm and leg rather than two of each.

Gorbachev's current attempt to combine the Ryzhkov and Shatalin plans scores poorly when viewed in this light. Controls would remain on prices of essential consumer goods, basic commodities like oil and gas, and other "key" goods and services, such as transportation and communications. Budgetary spending would be curtailed, but subsidies for many enterprises would be maintained. State enterprises are intended to be privatized, but no timetable or operational plan for doing so is established. Convertibility of the ruble is to be "gradual," without any indication of when or how.

By way of contrast, Poland's efforts at systemic transformation have been much more far-reaching than what is planned in the Soviet Union. Yet even Poland's changes have been insufficiently inclusive. On the positive side, fiscal discipline has been imposed and the budget deficit has been reduced from approximately 8 percent to 1 percent of GNP. Monetary discipline has been encouraged by separating the Central Bank from the Treasury. Ninety percent of all prices have been decontrolled, and convertibility of the zloty has been maintained at a stable rate since January 1990, with exports increasing, hard currency imports declining, and a resulting trade surplus of over $2 billion.

These are significant accomplishments, but they are not sufficient. To date, the Poles have only partially privatized. They have deferred the breaking up of state monopolies and delayed the wage reform necessary to create proper incentives for workers and managers. Hence, supply responses and sectoral resource reallocations have been inhibited, and output, employment, and inflation have suffered.

Still, if transformation to a market system is more tractable and the attendant costs are lower than is commonly assumed, why has progress been lacking (as in the Soviet Union), or limited (as in Poland)?

The question is genuinely puzzling. Part of the answer may be that many members of the unusually diverse chorus of ex-communists, socialists, social democrats, and erstwhile central planners, who intone free market rhetoric, are often decidedly ambivalent about the desirability of real transformation. So they seek reasons or excuses for delaying and temporizing, even while solemnly acknowledging the necessity for eventual systemic change.

November 1990

32

Democracy and Free Markets

When Boris Yeltsin visits Washington in the middle of June, his hosts will encourage, if not urge, him to proceed aggressively with both democratization and marketization in Russia. Yet the frequent, sometimes bitter and surely recurring disputes between Yeltsin and the Russian parliament are a reminder that the relationship between democratization and marketization is more complex, less predictable, and more conflicted than is often assumed. Contrary to the familiar rhetoric of U.S. policy statements, Congressional legislation, and media pronouncements, "democracy" and "free markets" are not synonymous.

To be sure, the two have several significant features in common. Both involve decentralization, devolution, and competition. Free markets decentralize and devolve economic power among competing producers and competing consumers. Democracy decentralizes and devolves political power among competing parties, candidates, and voters.

Nevertheless, the connection between them is not assured. Some democratic polities, like Israel and India, have socialist rather than market-oriented economies. And some market-oriented economies have (or have had for protracted periods) authoritarian, nondemocratic polities—for example, South Korea from 1960 through the 1980s, Chile in the 1970s and 1980s, and Singapore, Taiwan, and South China currently.

Reflecting on the relation between democracy and free markets, some (Hayek, Friedman) have argued that the two are mutually dependent and inextricably connected—each requires the other. Others (Lipset) have suggested that the relationship between the two, while mutually supportive, is not determinative—one may occur without the other. And still others (Schumpeter) have argued that the relationship between markets and democracy may well be competitive and conflicting.

The formidable obstacles that the Russian parliament presents for Yeltsin's economic reforms reflect the sometimes conflicted relationship between markets and democracies, but the underlying reasons differ from those which worried Schumpeter. Schumpeter saw the conflict between democracy and free markets arising from the opposing tendencies associated with each of them: on the one hand, the tendency of free market processes to generate large disparities between winners and losers; and, on the other hand, the tendency of democratic processes to take from the winners and redistribute their gains—in the process undermining incentives and substituting central controls and regulations in place of free markets.

Yeltsin's problem is of a different, but not unrelated sort. It springs from the process of transforming a nonmarket, command economy into a market economy at the same time as an authoritarian political system is being transformed into a more democratic one. In Russia's case, the conflict arises because the market transformation requires that several essential, as well as interacting, measures must be implemented simultaneously, or at least in close synchronization with one another. These measures involve fiscal and monetary stabilization (a balanced budget and control of the money supply); decontrol of prices and wages; privatization, demonopolization, and free entry of competing new enterprises; currency convertibility; and a suitable social safety net. The monetary and fiscal controls provide the stable macroeconomic environment that enables the microeconomic incentives and mechanisms of the other measures to move resources to more efficient and growth-promoting uses. Because these measures are synergistically connected, the chance that any one will be effective is reduced in the absence of reciprocal support provided by the others.

The rub lies in the unsurprising, although not inevitable, tendency of more or less democratically selected legislatures (the present Russian parliament lies in the "less democratic" part of this range) to delay, obstruct, and restrict implementation of comprehensive marketizing reforms, and to do so in concert with special interest constituencies. In Russia, these special interests reside in the state enterprises, especially the military-industrial complex, and the bureaucracy—both of which correctly anticipate that they would be big losers in a genuinely free market environment.

Yeltsin has demonstrated remarkable adroitness and political sophistication in coping with these pressures—maintaining at least modest progress toward marketization, while being obliged periodically to backtrack in response to resistance and threats from the so-called "conservative" forces in the Russian parliament. This backtracking is reflected by the recent decisions of the Gaidar government to postpone privatization, to continue large subsidies to nonproductive (and often counterproductive) state enterprises, and to maintain huge budget deficits that add to a continually expanding money supply and thereby intensify inflationary pressures.

Where this will lead is unclear. As Sam Goldwyn observed, forecasts are always hazardous—especially about the future.

However, it is doubtful that progress by this oscillatory process—one step backward for every two steps forward—will be sufficient to move the ossified Russian economy toward an effectively functioning market system.

In a Panglossian world, democratization and free markets would progress in step and in harmony, or at least in measured and balanced counterpoint to one another. There would be a "trade-on," rather than a trade-off, between them. Moreover, in the long run the association between democracy and free markets is more assured than in the intervening short runs that comprise it. But in the pressing short run that Yeltsin and his supporters confront, difficult choices may well arise between the demands of market economics and the restraints imposed by democratic politics. Yeltsin's choices may, in turn, face Western policymakers with a dilemma: accepting an abridgement of Russia's inchoate democratization (for example, if Yeltsin's authority to govern by decree is expanded) to sustain the economy's embryonic marketization, or opposing such a trade-off. Neither alternative is without drawbacks, but watchful acceptance is preferable because opposition will probably not advance either democracy or free markets.

June 1992

33

Some Hopeful Signs amidst the Commonwealth's Economic Travails

With the remarkably swift establishment of the Commonwealth of Independent States (CIS) on December 21, 1991, the leaders of its member republics should be able to turn their attention from politics to economics. Expecting the worst, they may have reason to be encouraged by what they find. While there is no doubt that the economies of the republics—especially Russia and Ukraine—are in trouble, considerable doubt is warranted that the actual trouble is as deep and dire as asserted by numerous recent alarmist pronouncements.

These forebodings have included forecasts by Eduard Shevardnadze that the gross national product will decrease to half its 1990 level, by Secretary Baker that we may be seeing "the economy collapse with no bottom in sight," and by *Pravda* that "total pauperization of the people and final collapse of the monetary system" impend.

Official Soviet data from the State Statistics Commission (GOSKOM-STAT) and from published CIA figures, which underlie the foregoing prophesies, are also profoundly pessimistic. These sources estimate a fall in GNP of 15 percent in 1991 and forecast a further decline in 1992 of 20 percent or more.

These gloomy assessments result, in considerable part, from the shortcomings of the official statistics, as well as from observation of the bare shelves in state stores. But these are imperfect and unreliable indicators because transactions are increasingly taking place outside the official distribution channels. Consequently, the official statistics are of limited help in tracking the economic activity that is occurring in the wake of erosion of the superstructure of the former command system, and appearance of the early signs of an emerging market economy.

One of the striking ironies in the current situation is that the official data, which in the past substantially and perennially *overestimated* the size and performance of the Soviet economy, are probably now substantially *underestimating* the economic condition of the principal republic economies. Moreover, the previous overestimates have contributed to exaggerated estimates of how far the economy must have fallen to get to its present position. Not having been where it was believed to be, the economy appears to have fallen farther to arrive where it presently is!

For marketization to proceed, one of the quintessential requisites is removal of the bureaucratic command structure that formerly prevented, and more recently has distorted, the operation of market forces. Much of the current economic disarray reflects this process—a process that can be likened to what Joseph Schumpeter characterized, in another context, as "creative destruction." As the process proceeds, economic activity has gravitated away from the former official economy and toward the "second" or "underground" economy. What were initially "leakages" from the official economy have become streams that eventually will become a flood to the former second economy as this becomes the real economy of the republics. Marketization in the CIS republics can be plausibly viewed as a process in which the gray and black markets become open and official, thus displacing the former nonmarket command system.

Evidence of this process is inevitably incomplete and anecdotal, but nonetheless significant.

As the previously existing long-haul distribution systems have become sundered, localized economic activities and new channels of production and distribution have begun to appear. More than four hundred commodity exchanges have developed to facilitate such local activities, often through barter transactions. As David Brooks has observed (*Wall Street Journal*, December 10, 1991), "entrepreneurs are sprouting up like weeds." There are also frequent instances where enterprises—both military and nonmilitary ones—are devoting overtime shifts to producing output for payment in kind to employees and for barter exchange on the gray or black markets. And there are indications that some of the principal republics' external trade—imports as well as exports—is taking place outside official reporting channels.

Most if not all of these types and signs of burgeoning economic activity are omitted from the official data collection.

This is not to say that the economic picture is rosy in Russia, Ukraine, and the other republics of the CIS, especially in certain of their key urban centers: the shelves of state stores are bare, prices on the unofficial markets have soared, and the ruble has been debased by enormous expansion of the money supply. Nor does it deny that some forms of external assistance may be of high priority in special circumstances—including assistance to establish more reliable means for measuring economic activity in general and progress in particular. But it does suggest that the repeated assertions and forecasts of unrelieved decline and glooms are exaggerated and unconvincing because they are based on misleadingly incomplete data.

It also suggests that the prospects for success of Boris Yeltsin's initial package of economic reforms—notably, price and wage decontrol combined with fiscal (and, one hopes, monetary) stabilization—may be brighter than is commonly assumed, and that these prospects may be improved by the growth of market-oriented economic activity that is already under way.

January 1992

34

Limited Optimism Rather Than Boundless Pessimism About the Russian Economy

The current consensus among putative experts places the Russian economy's prospects as somewhere between poor and dismal. But the consensus may be wrong. To be sure, there are legitimate reasons for the prevailing pessimism. However, there are other reasons that lead to more optimism, or at least less pessimism, than the consensus implies.

The principal concerns contributing to the gloomy assessment include: the insufficiency of economic reform measures undertaken by President Boris Yeltsin and Acting Prime Minister Yegor Gaidar, the sharp declines reported in Russian GNP and employment, the sustained and growing budget and "off-budget" deficits, the consequent risk of hyperinflation, and the enormous unresolved problems of converting Russian military industry to civil pursuits.

The insufficiencies of the Yeltsin-Gaidar reforms stand out clearly when compared with what needs to be done. Transforming Russia's command economy into a market-oriented one requires implementation of six essential and mutually reinforcing measures: fiscal and monetary stabilization (a balanced budget and control of the money supply); decontrol of prices and wages; assuring property rights, privatization, demonopolization, and free entry of competing new enterprises; currency convertibility; and a suitable social safety net. The interactions among these measures mean that the effectiveness of any one will be reduced if the others are not in train.

Viewed in this light, the Yeltsin-Gaidar program has indeed been modest. It has concentrated on price and wage decontrol combined with fiscal and monetary stabilization efforts. And even these limited efforts have been associated with insufficient implementation by the bureau-

177

cracy, as well as backtracking by government in response to resistance and opposition from the so-called "conservative" forces in the Russian parliament. Contrary to its previously announced policy, the government has been obliged to extend large subsidies to unproductive state enterprises, resulting in budget deficits that add to a continually expanding money supply.

The inadequacy of Gaidar's efforts to bring about macroeconomic stabilization is reflected by the mounting Russian budget deficit, which reached over 120 billion rubles during the first five months of 1992. For 1992 as a whole, the deficit will be about 17 percent of the Russian GNP. (In comparison, the swollen U.S. federal government budget deficit is less than 6 percent of U.S. GNP.) Worries about the possibility of hyperinflation are also evoked by the enormous increase of over two trillion rubles in interenterprise credits.

Moreover, with regard to another important dimension of reform, progress toward privatization and demonopolization of state industry has been virtually nil.

Still another factor on the downside is the serious decline in Russian GNP, reported as 17 percent in 1991, with a drop of more than 25 percent estimated for 1992.

Thus, the reasons that underlie the pessimistic consensus are numerous and serious. But they tell only part of the story. There are other parts that are more encouraging.

First, consider the statistics purporting to show a sharp decline in Soviet GNP. It is ironic that the official data, which in the past perennially *overestimated* the size and performance of the then-Soviet economy, are now almost certainly *underestimating* the economic condition of Russia and the other principal republics. Indeed, the previous overestimates have contributed to exaggerated estimates of how far the economy has fallen to get to its present position. Not having been where it was believed to be, the economy appears to have fallen farther to arrive where it now is!

The official data on Russian real output are in error because they fail to cover much new economic activity—especially output of food and consumer goods—that deliberately evades official data collection agencies. One reason for the systematic underreporting is the desire of producers, especially new entrepreneurs, to avoid high government taxes—notably the 28 percent value-added tax, and the 32 percent business profits tax. As a result, prices in the flourishing black or gray markets are sometimes lower than those in Russian state stores!

Another reason for the systematic underreporting of real output is the use of equipment and input supplies by state enterprises for "moonlighting" production, which finds its way into "noninstitutional" (i.e., "black" or "gray") markets, including export markets. This results in under-invoicing or noninvoicing of some exports, and the accumulation of hard currency deposits that are held abroad. The latter represents a flight of capital whose repatriation to Russia will depend on creating an environment that makes its use in the domestic economy profitable.

Still another source of underreporting is the disruption of the previously existing long-haul distribution systems of the Soviet economy. As a result, localized economic activities and new channels of production and distribution have begun to appear. Hundreds of commodity exchanges have developed to facilitate such local transactions, often through barter, and sometimes involving the "moonlighted" production of both military and nonmilitary state enterprises.

Furthermore, to the extent that declines in real output have actually occurred, they are a misleading indicator of consumer well-being. Much of the declines represent reductions of military output, as well as output of producers' durable goods and heavy metallurgical industry, rather than of consumer goods.

Next, consider the budget deficit and the expanded monetary stock. This problem has probably also been exaggerated. For example, the enormous increase in inter-enterprise ruble credits represents a nominal increase in the monetary stock whose turnover velocity is low. Although there is a possibility that part of these huge "accounts receivable" will be monetized, this is likely to take place slowly and to have only a limited effect on the risk of hyperinflation.

Turning to the vital issue of property rights, privatization, and demonopolization of state industry, it is true that progress has been disappointingly slow. Nevertheless, the new privatization law promulgated at the end of June 1992, is encouraging. The law is intended to privatize 70 percent of all industrial assets and a higher proportion of total Russian manufacturing value-added, according to the chief economist of the powerful Association of Industrialists and Entrepreneurs, Yevgeny Yasin. The government's declared aim is to accomplish this goal within three years, although Yasin indicated to me in June his belief that it would (and should!) take longer. The law provides for privatization of state enterprises through various forms of stock distribution. These include an initial gift of 25 percent of the shares to enterprise workers, as well as sale of another 5 percent to managers at "book value" (an elusive standard because of the absence of a price system for assessing book value and depreciation). The remaining shares are to be available for purchase by workers and managers, as well as by Russian citizens using vouchers distributed to them. These shares will also be available for bidding by foreign investors at the enterprise auctions planned in the coming months.

It remains to be seen how well the privatization plan will be implemented. Ironically, the fact that it has already been criticized from all sides of the political and ideological spectrum is probably an encouraging sign of the plan's merit. For example, the staunchly promarket, free enterprise advocates on what in Russia is viewed as the liberal "left," criticize the plan because its targets are too low, its pace too slow, and its bureaucratic complexity too Byzantine. These critics include Larissa Piyasheva, Vasilii Selunin, and Boris Pinsker, among others. The plan is also criticized from the conservative "right"—for example by Arkadi Volsky and Yasin on behalf of the Association of Industrialists and Entrepreneurs—on the grounds that it is too ambitious, too rapid, and too rigid.

It is important to note that the intense differences among these competing views are associated with a key characteristic that should allow compromises to be worked out. This characteristic relates to the continuity, rather than discontinuity, of the underlying issues separating the reforming activists from the bureaucracy, as well as from the enterprise managers and workers. These issues include not only the pace and character of privatization, but also the other dimensions of systemic transformation—notably, monetary and fiscal stabilization, and price decontrol. All of these elements can be implemented more or less fully, and more or less rapidly. *They are inherently "more-or-less" in nature, rather than binary "all-or-nothing."* Political compromises are more likely than would be the case if the contending issues were binary because binary issues provide less of an opportunity for "splitting the difference" between contesting parties.

One important issue for the success of reform efforts, not only in Russia but in the other republics as well, involves the resumption of trade among the republics. The special importance of such trade derives from an unfortunate legacy of the Soviet command economy that established monopolies for production of particular equipment or other products in one or another republic. The aim of this misguided effort was to achieve economies of large-scale production. The actual result was to create critical interdependencies among the different republics and regions of the Soviet economy.

However, since dissolution of the Soviet Union in January 1992, trade channels among the republics have been disrupted, with seriously adverse repercussions for the separate economies, particularly those of Russian and Ukraine. For example, the Ukrainian economy had previously relied on crude oil, textiles, and metallurgical products from Russia, while the Russian economy imported food and some finished machinery and electronic products from Ukraine. These prior trade channels have been disrupted by the breakup of the Union. Prospects for removal of trade barriers among the republics are unclear, although the benefits from such opening would be enormous.

Here again there are signs that progress can be made through reasonable compromises. One encouraging indicator that the trade impasse can be resolved is the recent compromise between Russia and Ukraine over the highly explosive issue of responsibility for the Black Sea fleet, which both republics had previously claimed. In early August 1992, Russia and Ukraine agreed to share responsibility for command and operations of the fleet over the next three and a half years—a compromise that also augurs well for compromises on the trade issue.

Finally, the Russian economy's prospects are inevitably complicated by the enormously swollen scale of military industry in the economy. At least 25 percent of Soviet GNP was directly or indirectly accounted for by military industry, as well as a much larger fraction of high technology industry, and top quality human and physical inputs. How and how rapidly these resources are to be diverted to production for the civil sector will have serious consequences for the marketization and development of the Russian economy as a whole.

On the positive side, there is widespread consensus, as well as resignation, among managers of military industry on the necessity for deep reductions in military production, and conversion of industrial assets toward civilian production. The new privatization law, which will encompass some though not all parts of the Russian military industrial complex, is another encouraging sign. There are also innumerable examples and anecdotes about new joint ventures between elements of Russian military industry and foreign investors. For instance, one particular military enterprise that produced top quality guidance systems for the most advanced Soviet ICBM systems has both equipment and skilled personnel capable of producing top quality surgical equipment for eventual export on world markets. Despite such anecdotes, very little has been accomplished in military conversion.

Although most military industry assets will have to be redeployed or scrapped, the Russian economy will still probably maintain an appreciable military industrial base to support the future Russian military establishment, as well as to export on international arms markets. For effective conversion to proceed, what is needed is an opening and loosening of the government strictures that still confine military enterprises. The large assets they control should be available for redeployment to civilian uses by both new Russian entrepreneurs acting alone or in concert with foreign joint ventures.

In sum, there are positive and encouraging signs, as well as negative and discouraging ones. This is not a case where the glass is half full, nor is it one in which the glass is entirely empty. The Russian economy could encounter hyperinflation. The polity might experience a sharp swing to the right. And fragmentation and civil strife might occur within or among the republics of the Commonwealth of Independent States. On the other hand, reforms may proceed. Compromises may be made. And marketization may gain momentum and succeed.

Policies followed by the United States and the other G-7 governments can be of some help in contributing to a more favorable outcome, but this help will inevitably be limited. Though the symbolic as well as material importance of the West's $24 billion aid package should not be underestimated, the principal emphasis of Western efforts should be focused on facilitating private investment and trade: specifically, on accelerating Russian access to both the international capital market—perhaps with the assistance of government-financed investment guarantees—and to goods markets through the extension of most-favored-nation access by the U.S. and European Community markets.

But the decisive role will not be played by the West. It will be played by the Russians, and they know it. In the midst of all the heated controversies in Russian political and economic circles, that recognition itself is an encouraging sign—a sign that warrants moderate optimism rather than boundless pessimism about the Russian economy's prospects.

January 1993

35

Two are Better Than One

On December 1, the Ukrainian electorate will probably endorse by a large majority a democratic referendum establishing the Republic's sovereign independence. Notwithstanding the pending referendum, as well as Ukraine's decision two weeks ago to sign a broad, although vague, economic cooperation treaty with nine other republics of the former Soviet Union (FSU) a central question remains unresolved: Precisely what economic relationships should be sought between the two principal republics, Russia and Ukraine, which together comprise 70 percent of the FSU's population and 80 percent of its gross product? The options range from sharp separation to close economic linkage between the two republics.

In sorting out the advantages and disadvantages of each option, as well as considering whether the United States should favor or deliberately avoid favoring either one, there is merit in reflecting on what would be in the best economic interests of Russia and Ukraine. Contrary to much of the conventional wisdom, separate and sovereign economic status would be economically preferable for both republics.

Prospects for economic improvement in both Russia and Ukraine will be enhanced by rapid and inclusive marketization of their command economies. In turn, marketization depends on the simultaneous, or at least contemporaneous, implementation of six essential reforms. And implementation of these reforms is more likely if the two republics have economically separate status.

The essential reforms include: monetary reform to ensure control of the money supply and credit; fiscal control to assure budgetary balance and to limit monetization of a budget deficit if one occurs; price and wage deregulation to link prices and wages to costs and productivity, respectively; privatization, legal protection of property rights, and the break-up of state monopolies (including defense industry); a social "safety net" to protect those who may become unemployed; and currency convertibility to link the transforming economies to the world economy and to competition in international markets.

The first two elements (monetary reform and fiscal control) and the fifth (the social safety net) create the broad macroeconomic environment that enables the incentive mechanisms of the other three to move resources toward more efficient and growth-promoting uses.

The proposals that Boris Yeltsin has recently induced the Russian parliament to accept include most of these essential elements. The challenge and uncertainty lie in their implementation.

Separate economic status for the Russian and Ukrainian republics will improve prospects for implementation. And the several components of marketizaton will be advanced by this status.

With respect to implementation, less bureaucratic interference and delays can be expected if the republics are economically separate rather than joined. One reason relates to the diseconomies of scale in large bureaucracies: a bureaucracy that covers both Ukraine and Russia will simply be bigger, more cumbersome, and less flexible than a smaller one. A second reason is that marketization will be able to proceed more rapidly if it is separate from the ethnic and nationalistic overtones and second-guessing that is likely to ensue if Russia and Ukraine are closely linked.

Furthermore, separate and independent republics would provide greater room for experimentation with different modalities of reform. For example, there isn't a single demonstrably preferable mode of privatization. It should be possible to experiment with several different modes if the units are smaller rather than the enormous one that would result from closely linking Russia and Ukraine.

With respect to the specific components of marketization, *fiscal and monetary control* is probably easier to accomplish if the implementing units are smaller. *Price and wage deregulation* will be neither more nor less difficult if the two republics are separate or joined. As noted above, *property rights and privatization* are areas for active experimentation with alternative modes, and this should be easier to do in small rather than large political jurisdictions. The *social safety net* may be one area in which a larger economic entity rather than two smaller ones is preferable because it would provide more opportunity for spreading risk (analogous to hedging by portfolio diversification). In any event, however,

Ukraine should be large enough on this count, even if it is only a third the size of the Russian republic.

Finally, with respect to *currency convertibility*, prospects for moving in this direction are better if the two republics are separate, each with its own floating but convertible rate. Ukraine can probably aspire to achieve this more quickly than either Russia alone, or the two republics together.

To be sure, numerous economic arguments have been advanced against separation and in favor of close linkage between Ukraine and Russia. But these arguments are unconvincing.

One argument is that the Russian and Ukrainian republics should be closely joined because they are economically interdependent as a result of decades of monopolistic industries located in each area. The short rebuttal to this is simply free trade between the republics. This, combined with rapid movement toward price and wage deregulation within both republics, will be necessary to uncover the realities of comparative costs that have been obscured by command prices.

Second, is the argument that it will be more difficult to divide the $80 billion of external Soviet debt if the republics are entirely separate from one another. But this misses the point: the real burden of debt servicing will inevitably be the subject of dispute and negotiation among different parts of the FSU, whether the republics are integrated or separate.

A third argument is that convertibility will be harder to establish if there are two separate Ukrainian and Russian currencies. This argument is also flawed. If both currencies are convertible, convertibility between them is established, q.e.d. If, on the other hand, only one is convertible, then at least the process of reform has advanced in that singular case.

In sum, two are better than one! If the United States chooses, for political reasons, not to take a position in favor of separation of the two republics, it should, for economic reasons, at least avoid favoring a close linkage between them.

November 1991

36

The Question of Soviet Aid

Aid to the Soviet Union was initially placed on the agenda of the G-7 Summit in Houston in 1990 by France and Germany. It was elevated to the top of the G-7 agenda in London in 1991 by Gorbachev's own appearance there. In the wake of the global euphoria over the aborted seventy-two-hour Moscow coup, the subject has acquired immediate prominence.

Although Gorbachev received less at the London meeting than he asked for, he did not leave empty handed. He was offered technical assistance to help move the Soviet Union toward a market economy, a recommendation by the G-7 for associate (nonborrowing) Soviet membership in the International Monetary Fund and the World Bank, and (from George Bush) the prospect of most-favored-nation access to the U.S. market. He also elicited an implied promise: "full engagement" (implying Western aid) by the G-7 members would depend on clear evidence of Soviet progress in implementing an "irrevocable commitment" to fundamental systemic reform.

Despite its ambiguity, this promise will surely be tested in the coming months, as well as at the 1992 G-7 Summit in Berlin. The ensuing debate will probably strain the Seven's cohesion by pitting its European members against Japan and the United States.

Japan's role is crucial because Japan is the only member of the Seven with a substantial and continuing current account surplus—probably about $50 to $60 billion in 1991—that would enable it to finance large-scale aid. (The German and U.S. current account deficits will be about $25 and $50 billion, respectively.) If G-7 members other than Japan were to provide aid to the Soviet Union, they would be obliged—directly or indirectly—to borrow from Japan, or to sell other assets to it in return for current Japanese funding. Japan would be the ultimate paymaster.

Although Japan's stance would doubtless be heavily influenced by the United States, its reluctance to become "fully engaged" in aiding the Soviet Union has deep roots. They relate not only to its unresolved claims for return by the Soviets of the four Kurile Islands, but to other concerns as well: the powerful and still modernizing Soviet military forces—especially naval, air, and missile forces—in the Okhotsk bastion and in Soviet East Asia; the changing but still uncertain state of Soviet relations with North and South Korea; and the serious Japanese doubts about whether there are realistic prospects of achieving successful economic and political reform in the Soviet Union.

On all of these matters, Japan is the most "conservative" of all the G-7 countries in its coolness toward large-scale aid to the Soviet Union.

The case for large-scale aid from the West entails other fundamental shortcomings, quite apart from Japan's crucial role, and notwithstanding the abundant good will toward the Soviet people and Boris Yeltsin generated by their stalwart resistance to the short-lived Moscow coup.

First, the proposition that concessional government-to-government aid can assist in transforming a nonmarket system into a market one is an oxymoron. The essence of a market system is that inputs (labor, capital, raw materials) and outputs (goods and services) are exchanged at prices determined by the interaction between market demand and supply. Prices of outputs reflect their scarcity values and production costs, and prices of inputs reflect their productivity (or "opportunity cost") in their best alternative uses.

The essence of concessional aid, on the other hand, is that capital, equipment, and commodities are provided by donors at prices that do not reflect market forces. Government-to-government aid carries with it either no costs or subsidized costs to the recipient, thereby absolving it from having to meet a market test in the use of aid. Whereas genuine marketizing reform requires market-based prices, "aid" means that market prices are deliberately ignored. While marketization implies access to external resources through the competitive international capital market, "aid" implies access through the favors of foreign governments.

To promote marketization by concessional aid is like teaching a child to avoid fires by giving her matches, or reforming an alcoholic by a gift of liquor.

The second flaw is the unavoidable problem of resource fungibility. Providing the Soviet Union with aid resources means that donors cannot be sure what the net effect actually is of the additional resources that are provided. An ostensible "bargain" that purports to relate the added resources to changes in Soviet resource allocations—for example, to cuts in Soviet military spending and forces, as advocated by Martin Feldstein—or to other changes in Soviet behavior, would be an illusory bargain. The reason is that Soviet policymakers already face strong and growing pressures to cut military allocations—pressures that will no doubt be intensified by the recently aborted coup—to scale back or divest the capacity of military industry and to shift it to market-based civil production. Because resources are fungible, concessional assistance will be as likely to abate as to abet these pressures.

Another reason why concessional aid is as likely to hinder as help the necessary reform process is that such aid would inevitably be provided to the Union government, whereas prospects for genuine reform are clearly much better in the Republics. One of the sobering lessons of all U.S. experience with foreign aid from the Marshall Plan to current aid to developing countries is that government-to-government aid strengthens the central government at the expense of the periphery. Hence, notwithstanding the 9-plus-1 Union Treaty, foreign aid to the central Soviet government is bound to strengthen its hand in dealing with the republics, thereby militating against genuine reform.

One version of the argument for large-scale aid that will probably surface in the coming months focuses on its potentially appealing role in providing a "stabilization reserve" to underwrite convertibility of the ruble. This, too, is flawed. If and as monetary and fiscal balance is attained in the Soviet Union, convertibility with a floating exchange rate can be established with only minimal hard currency reserves. If this balance is not attained, the ensuing run on the stabilization reserve would rapidly exhaust it, thereby aborting convertibility.

With appropriate reform measures, aid will not be needed. Without it, aid will be wasted. Large-scale concessional aid to the Soviet Union is an idea that should be interred before it is revived. It is neither something that the West should promise, nor that those who seek genuine reform in the Soviet Union should be encouraged to expect.

September 1991

37

Aiding Russia and Ukraine

Although Presidents Clinton and Mitterand, and former President Nixon agree on the importance of foreign assistance to Russia, neither they nor other advocates have been specific about how much or what types of aid are appropriate. To the limited extent that specifics have been addressed, doubts are warranted about their feasibility or merit.

In addressing the aid question, several considerations are salient:

First, prior Western aid has elicited mixed, but mainly unfavorable, reactions within Russia. Criticisms, by supporters as well as opponents of Boris Yeltsin, have focused on both the small amounts (far below the $24 billion promised by the G-7 a year ago), as well as the added debt burden this aid has imposed on the already beleaguered Russian economy. Moreover, Western aid to Russia has elicited reactions in Ukraine that are even more unfavorable than those in Russia itself. While Russians view Western aid to date as niggardly, Ukrainians view it invidiously because of what they see as the total neglect of Ukraine's own needs and interests.

Second, future aid from the West should be cognizant of the Hippocratic precept to do no harm ("...abstain from whatever is deleterious"). In economies like those of Russia and Ukraine that are trying to become more marketized and are beginning to generate and respond to market price signals, foreign subsidies provided through government-to-government aid channels may nullify those signals, thereby retarding rather than advancing marketization.

Finally, aid should be *purposeful rather than personal*: it should seek to advance purposes and policies linked to the fundamentals of transforming the economies and societies of Russia and Ukraine. While President Yeltsin is eminently deserving of encouragement and support, foreign aid policies should not be so narrowly or personally conceived that their rationale lapses if the Yeltsin government proves to be transitory.

A four-part foreign assistance package, that comports with these considerations, would consist of: (1) debt relief through rescheduling and cancellation of some foreign debt, and swapping some of the remaining debt for equities in state enterprises undergoing privatization; (2) stimulating foreign direct investment in Russia and Ukraine by galvanizing the presently available OPIC investment insurance program, as well as by providing a stimulus to increase private, commercial insurance; (3) establishing a "market stabilizing mechanism" for global arms sales to assure Russia and Ukraine a "reasonable" share of the global arms market; and (4) supplementing the $800 million already appropriated for the dismantling of nuclear weapons with additional funds for these and related purposes.

Restructuring and Swapping Foreign Debt

Russia, Ukraine, and six other republics agreed, upon dissolution of the Soviet Union at the end of 1991, to assume "joint and several" responsibility for servicing the entire Soviet external debt, much of which was accumulated preceding and during Mikhail Gorbachev's 1985-1991 tenure. This debt, together with the additional debt incurred in 1992 and 1993, currently is between $75 and 80 billion. Russia is the only republic that has attempted to meet this extremely onerous servicing obligation. During the next three years, from 1993 to 1995, the annual burden represented by servicing long-term, hard-currency debt alone, will be between $10 and 14 billion, thereby preempting between one-third and one-half of Russia's annual hard currency foreign exchange earnings.

Two measures can contribute significantly to easing this burden. The first would have the Western creditors (Germany, Italy, and the other West European countries are collectively owed 70 percent of the total, the U.S. only 5 percent) to forgive all or most of the debt incurred before the formal dissolution of the Soviet Union on January 1, 1992. Most of the creditors' banking institutions have already built up loss reserves in anticipation of this prospect, so the financial impact would be modest. Moreover, by linking the debt cutoff to the historic date of the Soviet Union's dissolution, debt forgiveness would avoid a precedent that other debtor countries might invoke in an effort to obtain equal concessions for themselves.

The second measure is to swap some of the remaining sovereign debt for equities in state enterprises undergoing privatization in Russia and Ukraine. Under the Russian privatization law adopted last year, 35,000 state enterprises are to be privatized over the next three years. The process, which is currently underway, calls for 25 percent of the shares to be given to enterprise workers and managers, 30 to 35 percent to be auctioned to Russia's 150 million citizens in exchange for ruble vouchers already distributed to them, and the remaining shares to be retained by the state. If some of these government-held shares were swapped for debt liabilities, the economic burden of meeting the fixed servicing obligations of debt would be replaced by more flexible servicing obligations that depend instead on the economic performance of equities. Moreover, foreign creditors who acquire these assets will have incentives to enhance their stakes by adding management skills, technology, and improved access to Western markets, as well as by new investment. As the value of the existing debt declines on the secondary debt market, creditors' incentives to engage in such swaps will increase. (Significantly, medium term Soviet debt that carried a 20 percent discount in the fall of 1992, currently carries a 50 percent discount!)

Encouraging Foreign Investment
by Expanding Risk Insurance

The United States already has a modest program to encourage foreign investment in Russia and Ukraine by providing subsidized insurance against investors' exposure to political risks of expropriation or violence. This insurance is written by a government agency—the Overseas Private Investment Corporation—for a premium that is less than half the cost of roughly comparable political risk insurance that is sometimes available in the commercial insurance market.

To date, OPIC has approved insurance applications for only 7 investments with a face value of $121 million for Russia and none for Ukraine, from an applications pool of 256 for Russia with a face value of $22 billion, and 39 for Ukraine with a face value of $1.7 billion. The limited scale of these approvals is due to many factors, including especially OPIC's understandable reluctance to increase the risks that American taxpayers would be exposed to if turmoil ensued in Russia or Ukraine and compensation to insured investors were required.

However, foreign aid directed toward encouraging private investment is a high-leverage form of aid for furthering market-oriented economic reform. Toward this end, foreign investment in Russia and Ukraine can be boosted in two ways: by galvanizing OPIC's existing activities by reducing the bureaucratic bottlenecks that impede it, and allowing a tax credit of, say, 50 percent of the premiums that *private* insurers receive from issuing risk insurance to U.S. investors in Russia and Ukraine.

Assuring Russia and Ukraine a Reasonable Share of the World Arms Market

International weapons sales accounted in the last half of the 1980s for 20 percent of the former Soviet Union's export earnings, compared to about 4 percent for the U.S. To be sure, we have a general interest in both damping down the arms market and in drastic downsizing of Russian and Ukrainian military industry. Reductions of over 60 percent in Russia's defense procurement spending are accomplishing this downsizing. However, we should also acknowledge that Russia and Ukraine have a critical need for hard currency exports, and their comparative advantage for realizing them lies in arms sales.

Provided that exports of potentially destabilizing weapons—like submarines, cruise missiles, or advanced sea and land mines—are controlled, the United States and the other principal weapons exporters (France, Britain, China, and Germany) should establish a cartel-like stabilizing mechanism for the conventional arms market that would envisage for Russia and Ukraine an appreciable share (say, 20 percent) of the $35 billion annual weapons market.

Dismantling Nuclear Weapons and Retrofitting Nuclear Reactors

In 1992, the U.S. provided $800 million of Defense Department appropriations for dismantling tactical nuclear weapons in Russia and Ukraine. Less than 5 percent of these funds have been expended thus far, due to logistic, contracting and organizational delays on both the U.S. and Russian sides. In addition to expediting the effective use and expenditure of these funds, the U.S. should adopt a proposal by Robert Ellsworth to expand this effort. This proposal would increase the $800 million fund to assist in further weapons dismantling, as well as in retrofitting with radiation-containment structures the several dozen Chernobyl-type nuclear reactors located in Russia, Ukraine and other former Soviet states, and dismantling the 300 power reactors on Russian nuclear submarines that are to be decommissioned under existing arms control agreements.

Economic reform and political transformation in Russia and Ukraine inevitably involve military issues, like arms sales and weapons dismantling, because of the distorted gigantism of the military sectors inherited from the Soviet economy. Consequently, an effective economic aid package should include components that address these matters, as well as furthering purposes like debt abatement and foreign investment promotion, that Presidents Yeltsin and Kravchuk endorse, but that transcend their personal tenures. Finally, an effective aid package should be realistic and feasible, and not promise more than can be delivered, as Western aid has sometimes done in recent years.

April 1993

38

To Privatize, Randomize

Privatization is the top priority on the agenda of the reforming economies of Poland, Czechoslovakia, and Hungary. And there is nearly unanimous agreement among the political leaders of these countries, as well as their technical advisors, that a drastic shift of ownership of state enterprises from government to private hands is essential if these economies are to become competitive, market-based systems. (Privatization is no less essential in the Soviet Union, but its endorsement is much more ambiguous among the Soviet leadership in Moscow than in several of the Soviet Republics, especially the Russian Republic.)

Despite widespread acceptance of the goal, there remains intense disagreement about the methods, mechanisms, and speed of accomplishing it. Underlying the disagreement are a series of issues and obstacles, some spurious and some serious. The obstacles can be surmounted by a process that is simple, understandable and practicable; namely, privatizing by randomizing!

Because of the disagreements about appropriate methods and speed, privatization has proceeded at a snail's pace. In Poland, less than 5 percent of the state enterprises (fewer than 150 out of an estimated 3100 state enterprises) have been privatized—only 7 in 1990—and about 75 percent of total industrial capacity remains in government hands. Moreover, much of the remaining 25 percent has resulted from the start-up of new ventures, rather than the privatization and break-up of the large established state enterprises. (Recently, Poland proposed a complex plan to privatize an additional 400 state enterprises by placing them in the hands of 20 investment funds, and providing to each of Poland's 27 million adult citizens one share in each fund. The plan remains to be debated and approved by the Polish parliament.) In the other East European countries, progress has been even slower and still more limited. In the Soviet Union, it has been negligible.

Government officials responsible for privatization in Eastern Europe extenuate their record by noting that Margaret Thatcher succeeded in denationalizing only a dozen state enterprises during her ten years as prime minister! But the comparison is inapt. The British effort sought to bring the previously nationalized airline, railway, and telecommunications companies toward a point of profitability before selling shares to the public on the London exchange—a goal that is neither necessary nor practicable for existing state enterprises in Eastern Europe. Furthermore, despite the nationalization efforts of Britain's previous Labor governments, the bulk of Britain's industrial capacity—probably more than 80 percent—was still privately owned when the Thatcher program of privatization began in the early 1980s. Finally, the British example is not one that Eastern Europe should follow for yet another reason: the British government has retained a so-called "golden share" in several of the denationalized industries enabling the government to exercise an ultimate veto if it chose to do so, even after privatization.

Another objection raised against privatization in Eastern Europe is the lack of a suitable basis for valuation of the state enterprises to be privatized. It is argued that, until market forces can determine prices of output, as well as the costs of labor and other key inputs, enterprise profitability cannot be evaluated, and thus suitable values cannot be established for privatizing enterprise assets.

This objection is spurious. It arises from a misconception about the meaning of privatization. Privatization is simply the vesting or assignment of property rights in private hands. Market valuation can facilitate the vesting process, but it is not essential. What is essential is an effective means for shifting ownership from state to private hands in the interests of improving incentives, efficiency, and productivity.

Another objection to rapid privatization is that many of the large holders of liquid capital in the Eastern European countries (and in the Soviet Union as well) are said to have previously been members of the Communist *nomenklatura*, black marketeers, or "mafiosi." Consequently, their prospective acquisition of state enterprises—through, say, an auction sale—would be politically unacceptable and socially inequitable.

Although there are legitimate grounds for this concern, they don't invalidate the case for privatization. To repeat, privatization requires neither liquid capital nor market valuation. Instead, it requires a mechanism for divesting ownership from the state and vesting it in private hands.

One method that has been proposed for accomplishing rapid privatization is to issue vouchers or coupons representing ownership shares to specified groups of enterprise "insiders" and "outsiders:" for example, 20 percent to workers and management as enterprise "insiders," 15 to 20 percent to state banks that are themselves being privatized, 20 percent to pension funds, 30 percent to new mutual funds, and the remainder to be retained by government for later sales as a market for stock shares develops. The "black box" character of these or other percentage assignments has led to criticism and resistance to this proposal on the grounds that it is both "technocratic" and "inequitable": technocratic because the choice of percentages is viewed as mechanistic and unintelligible; and inequitable because of suspicion that the small number of potentially profitable enterprises among the larger number of potential losers will be distributed to favored groups operating behind a veil of bureaucratic decision making.

By contrast, randomization provides a method of accomplishing rapid privatization, while avoiding these pitfalls.

"Privatizing by randomizing" means that all ownership shares of state enterprises would be distributed to the general public—except for, say, a 20 percent "inducement" package for each enterprise's own employees and management to enlist their support—by means of a national lottery. Ex ante, each citizen would have an equal chance of receiving shares of prospectively profitable enterprises, as well as of nonviable ones. The "equitableness" of the randomization process derives from the equality of each citizen's initial chance of receiving a valuable or a valueless asset. Randomization has the further advantage of simplicity and intelligibility. If administered honestly, randomization is a means of speeding privatization—of getting the large state enterprises into private hands so that market forces can move them toward more efficient use, toward break-up into smaller entities, or to liquidation. As privatization proceeds, enterprise managers will become responsible to private shareholders who may choose new management, or sell their shares to other buyers, or decide to sell off parts of the large industrial enterprises to new and smaller enterprises.

To be sure, privatization is only one step—albeit a tremendous one—toward efficiency. And it must be underwritten by an appropriate legal code that protects property rights and provides a means for resolving disputes about them.

Nevertheless, accelerating privatization by randomization through a national lottery can jump-start an essential but presently stalled part of the process of transforming centrally planned economies into genuine market systems.

July 1991

39

Swapping Debt for Equity in Russia

One of the major obstacles to improving performance of the Russian economy is the heavy burden of servicing $70 billion of inherited Soviet sovereign debt, much of it accumulated during Mikhail Gorbachev's tenure from 1985 through 1991. The burden can be measurably eased by giving foreign creditors the option of swapping existing debt for equity shares in Russia's privatizing state enterprises. As a result, not only can the debt burden be eased, but a boost can be given to privatization and foreign investment, as well.

One month prior to the Soviet Union's formal dissolution on January 1, 1992, Russia, Ukraine, and six other republics of the former Soviet Union agreed to assume "joint and several" responsibility for servicing the entire Soviet external debt. The understanding was that Russia would provide 60 percent of the annual servicing payments, although in principle each of the signatories assumed full liability if other signatories failed to meet their shared obligations. In fact, Russia is the only republic currently in compliance with these obligations.

The large annual servicing burden, currently $9 billion, represents 30 percent of Russia's annual foreign exchange earnings, and about one half of the annual net foreign loans and grants announced by the G-7, but not yet fully disbursed to the Commonwealth republics. In effect, the G-7 donors, including the International Monetary Fund and World Bank, are paying with one hand, while withdrawing with the other—in the process, adding to the debt burden that Russia and the other republics will face in the future.

This smoke-and-mirrors artifice recalls the Latin American debt predicament in the 1980s, which gave rise to the Baker Plan in 1985 and the Brady Plan in 1989. These plans called for debt-equity swaps to ease the heavy debt burden and to promote privatization reform in Latin America, especially in Brazil, Mexico, and Argentina. (Actually, both the Baker and Brady Plans were foreshadowed by earlier proposals of Kiichi Miyazawa, then Japan's finance minister and currently its prime minister.) The ensuing swaps played a modest, but significant, role in converting Latin America's debt "crisis" into a more manageable, albeit still serious, financial problem. Moreover, some of the large Latin American creditors, such as Citicorp, that swapped debt for equities in the late 1980s realized very large profits from the subsequent resale of their equity acquisitions.

In Russia, the swap option could conceivably play a still more significant role than it did in Latin America. The privatization plans of Boris Yeltsin's government envisage conversion of a huge number of state enterprises into privatized, joint-stock companies. The magnitude and range of equities that can be put in play for debt conversion in Russia dwarfs what was available in Latin America. Although many of these enterprises have dubious prospects for survival, others are likely to be highly valuable, because they possess valuable assets, in such fields as fiber optics, electronics, propulsion, and metallurgy. Consequently, Russia's creditors, or their surrogates, should have a much wider and potentially more attractive range of opportunities and choices than were available in the Latin American precedent.

Russia's privatization law, promulgated in July 1992, calls for conversion of 70 percent of the assets of over 35,000 state enterprises to joint-stock ownership, over three years. To be sure, Russia's Union of Industrialists and Entrepreneurs, whose membership includes most of the larger enterprises, and its head, Arkady Volsky, argue that the privatization process should be reduced in scope and implemented more slowly than the law envisages. In any event, a massive privatization process will ensue even if the Volsky group manages to moderate its pace and scale.

The initial privatization *tranche* planned for December 1992 will market some 7,000 state enterprises, through several different channels: gifts of shares to enterprise workers (20 percent of the total shares) and managers (another 5 percent); privatization vouchers distributed to each of Russia's 150 million citizens, with a nominal face value of 10,000 rubles per voucher, accounting for 30 percent of the enterprises' shares; and the remaining 45 percent initially to be retained by government and available for subsequent sale.

These residual shares held by government provide the means for implementing a swap of some of the outstanding sovereign debt shouldered by Russia. Moreover, further down the road, the debt swaps can draw on a corresponding proportion of the more than 28,000 state enterprises that remain to be privatized in later phases of the process.

From the standpoint of Russia's foreign creditors (the principal one is Germany), the key question concerns the worth of the enterprises' stock. The answer is something between a puzzle and an enigma. In establishing the face value of each voucher at 10,000 rubles, the economists on Acting Prime Minister Yegor Gaidar's team based their estimates on the book-value of the 7,000 enterprises' assets recalculated in 1991 ruble prices. At these prices, the resulting 1.5 trillion ruble estimate represented perhaps $10 billion. Actually, the true market value of these assets is impossible to infer from these estimates both because the 1991 ruble prices were themselves not free market prices, and because even updated book values are imperfect indicators of the market values of the enterprises' assets.

In any event, the potential value of the assets that might be involved in debt swaps—including land, structures, equipment, and the human capital associated with the enterprises—may be large enough to make an appreciable contribution to easing the burden imposed by the existing foreign debt. To implement the debt-for-equity idea requires that two domains of Russian policymaking that have hitherto proceeded along more or less separate paths, should be closely linked—namely, privatization under Deputy Prime Minister Anatoli Chubais, and foreign debt servicing and rescheduling under Deputy Prime Minister Alexander Shokhin. Both foreign creditors and the Russian economy can thereby benefit.

Creditors can benefit from the opportunity of exchanging assets whose value will probably depreciate for assets that have a potential for appreciation. To be sure, the creditors will face a challenge of sifting a large volume of diverse equities whose future market value may be quite uncertain. But the creditors also know that the value of the sovereign Russian debt that they hold is itself highly uncertain. This debt currently trades at a 20 percent discount in the secondary debt market—and this discount is bound to increase as Russian efforts to reschedule the debt proceed, and as servicing payments predictably lag. Consequently, equity swaps may be relatively attractive despite the uncertainty of the equities' value, because the alternative of retaining debt will become decreasingly attractive to creditors.

The Russian economy can also realize significant benefits through the swaps. The economy's servicing burden will be eased by exchanging assets carrying fixed obligations for those whose servicing depends on asset performance. Moreover, foreign creditors who acquire these assets, or their subsequent purchasers, will have incentives to enhance their stakes by adding management skills, technology, improved access to western markets, and new investment, thereby contributing to the Russian economy's development and reform.

November 1992

Index